POLITICAL REALITIES
Edited on behalf of the Politics Associ[...]
Derek Heater

The Evolving Civil Service

Robert Pyper

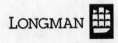

LONGMAN

For Elinor

Longman Group UK Limited
Longman House, Burnt Mill, Harlow, Essex, CM20 2JE, England
and Associated Companies throughout the World.

© Longman Group UK Limited 1991

First published 1991
ISBN 0 582 35568 0

*Set in 10/12pt Times, Linotron 202
Produced by Longman Singapore Publishers Pte Ltd
Printed in Singapore*

British Library Cataloguing in Publication Data

Pyper, Robert
  The evolving Civil Service. – (Politic realities)
  I. Title II. Series
  354.41006

  ISBN 0 582 35568 0

Contents

Abbreviations

CCSU	Council of Civil Service Unions
Cmnd	Command Paper
CPRS	Central Policy Review Staff
CSD	Civil Service Department
CSPCS	Civil Service Pay and Conditions of Service (Code)
DHSS	Department of Health and Social Security
DoE	Department of the Environment
DSS	Department of Social Security
DTI	Department of Trade and Industry
DWC	Departmental Whitley Councils
FCO	Foreign and Commonwealth Office
FMI	Financial Management Initiative
GCHQ	Government Communications Headquarters
IT	Information Technology
MINIS	Management Information System for Ministers
MoD	Ministry of Defence
MSC	Manpower Services Commission
NAO	National Audit Office
NWC	National Whitley Council
PAC	Public Accounts Committee
PAR	Programme Analysis and Review
PCA	Parliamentary Commissioner for Administration
PSA	Property Services Agency

1 Introduction

The size, role and functioning of the civil service in the British system of government have become central topics for political and academic debate in recent years. The key factors governing the relationship between civil servants and their ministers, and between the civil service as an institution and Parliament, have been picked over and analysed by politicians and commentators alike in the wake of events such as the prosecution of Clive Ponting and the leaking of official material during the Westland affair.

'To whom are civil servants ultimately accountable?' 'How should they react when torn between loyalty to their employers and a duty to act in the public interest?' There have been times when it seemed as if everyone from the Prime Minister and the Leader of the Opposition down to the university and school student taking examinations in government and politics needed to have clear answers to questions of this kind.

Similarly, the structure, organisation and management of the civil service have become topics of significant political and academic, as well as administrative, importance. The activities of crusading reformers, transferred from the high street stores and multinational corporations to the Whitehall corridors, have obliged those who wish to understand the changing political reality of British central government to turn their attention to the world of private business as well as the system of government.

In precise terms, what is this civil service which forms the focus for such interest and inquiry? The civil service with which we shall be concerned in this book can be simply defined.

- Most obviously, it is the 'civil' as opposed to the military or armed service of the state.
- It employs those servants of the Crown who are not holders of judicial or ministerial office.

1

- Technically, our focus of interest is the *home* civil service, as opposed to the diplomatic corps or overseas service. Nonetheless, for the purposes of brevity, we shall refer to the institution we examine simply as the civil service.

Civil servants make up about 2 per cent of the working population of the United Kingdom and approximately 10 per cent of all public sector employees.[1] Many public services, including health, education, the personal social services and policing, are delivered by public servants who are not part of the civil service, although they will depend upon civil servants for the provision of administrative and managerial support. Since 1976, when a total of 748,000 people worked in the civil service, staff numbers have fallen almost continuously, reaching 569,215 in 1989.

Industrial civil servants (one in eight in 1989) have formed a steadily declining proportion of the total since the 1950s, as some tasks performed by this group have been discontinued, altered, or privatised. Approximately three-quarters of all industrial civil servants are employed within the Ministry of Defence, in capacities such as firemen, cleaners, messengers, electricians, fitters and carpenters.

Our main concern will be with the non-industrial civil service. Those in this category are engaged in a wide variety of tasks, ranging from the provision of central administrative support and policy advice, to the direct delivery of services to the public via Job Centres, Tax Offices, and Social Benefit Offices, to name but three.

Figure 1.1: Home civil service (non-industrial) grades

Open Structure

Grade 1: Permanent Secretary
Grade 2: Deputy Secretary
Grade 3: Under Secretary
Grade 4: 'Executive Directing Bands' (and corresponding
              Professional and Scientific grades)
Grade 5: Assistant Secretary (and corresponding grades)
Grade 6: Senior Principal (and corresponding grades)
Grade 7: Principal (and corresponding grades)

Administration Group†

Senior Executive Officer
Higher Executive Officer (D)
Higher Executive Officer
Administration Trainee
Executive Officer
Administrative Officer*
Administrative Assistant*

Social Security Group

Local Officer 1
Local Officer 2

*'Clerical Officer' until January 1987.

Inland Revenue Group

Inspector of Taxes
Revenue Executive
Revenue Officer
Revenue Assistant

Professional and Technology Group

Senior P&T Officer
Higher P&T Officer
P&T Officer

Science Group

Senior Scientific Officer
Higher Scientific Officer
Scientific Officer
Assistant Scientific Officer

Other Grades

Personal Secretary
Typist
Prison Grade VII
Prison Grade VIII
Instructional Officer 1

Economist Group†

Senior Economic Assistant
Economic Assistant

Information Officer Group†

Senior Information Officer
Information Officer
Assistant Information Officer

Librarian Group†

Senior Librarian
Librarian
Assistant Librarian

Statistician Group†

Senior Assistant Statistician
Assistant Statistician

Training/Instructional Officer Group

Legal Category

Museums Category

Police Category

Research Category

†These Groups all fall within the 'General Category'.

Officials in this category are employed in a number of distinct Groups, including the Administration Group, which accounts for 45 per cent of non-industrial civil servants (see Figure 1.1 and Appendix 2). At the top of the grading system is the Open Structure, to which, in theory at least, there is access from all the occupational Groups. The Open Structure contains those we would normally think of as the Whitehall officials, although it should be noted that only 4 per cent of all non-industrial civil servants are graded at the top levels.

There are very wide variations in the sizes of the departments of state within which civil servants work (see Appendix 1). For example, the largest department, the Ministry of Defence, employs a total of 141,317 civil servants, while only 1,619 work in the Cabinet Office. Similarly, departments differ considerably in terms of the deployment of their staffs between Whitehall and other locations, as the following examples show:

Staff (industrial and non-industrial) located in Inner London (%)

Ministry of Defence	7.3
Department of Energy	81.3
Scottish Office	0.4
Treasury	56.8
All departments	13.6

In this book we shall examine the minister–civil servant relationship, the role of Parliament as a scrutineer of the bureaucratic machine, ethical and managerial issues, and, finally, the changing shape and purpose of departments of state. It would be impossible to do justice to such a task without first tracing the emergence of the modern civil service.

2 Historical Development of the Civil Service

The British civil service of the late twentieth century is a complex and sophisticated organisation. The modern institution contains within it certain characteristics and modes of operation which have their roots in earlier periods of British political history.

It is impossible to truly comprehend a system of government without reference to its historical development. As with the British constitution itself, the civil service is the product of a long process of evolution, within which key periods (especially periods of war) have witnessed significant bursts of innovation and reform. If we are to approach a proper understanding of the civil service as the twenty-first century approaches, it will be necessary for us to trace the evolutionary path to its origins, and identify the most important twists and turns along the way. We must also recognise that the process of evolution, by its very nature, continues even as we read!

1. Origins

It is now generally agreed that the British civil service began to emerge in its modern form from about the middle of the nineteenth century. However, it is possible to identify elements of what might loosely be described as a 'civil service' in earlier periods of history. It should be stressed, however, that the concept of a civil service is associated with reasonably advanced systems of government, and we should be wary of grafting modern terminology on to early modern or medieval structures.

Bearing this qualification in mind, it is possible to discern prototype 'civil servants', of various kinds, at different junctures in history. Take, for example, the small bands of educated clerics who were attached to the courts of the Anglo-Saxon kings.

When ordering a taxation or issuing a writ, the king would have consulted his secretariat. Edward the Confessor, like kings since Alfred at the latest, had a clerical staff of priests, headed by a chief clerk whose office developed into that of the medieval chancellor. One of their duties was to keep records: from the late Anglo-Saxon period comes evidence of very detailed surveys recording land-tenure, numbers of hides, and tax obligations.[1]

The coming of the Normans, and increased centralisation, led to a more sophisticated form of government. Officials, household servants and powerful barons provided the king with political and administrative support, looking after his monies and valuables as he travelled around, organising his household, and planning his military campaigns. By 1199 the chancery clerks were systematically keeping records of the king's correspondence. As it became increasingly impracticable for vast numbers of officials to travel with their kings, embryonic departments of government gradually began to settle in Whitehall. The frequent foreign and domestic conflicts of the Middle Ages were financed by regular taxation, which was managed by the bureaucracy of the king's Exchequer.

Financial management became the linch-pin of the government of Henry VII, the first Tudor monarch. Between 1485 and 1509 he

> attacked the problem of a creaking inherited machine unsuitable for his purposes by creating an alternative based on his own household .... The key official in this alternative machine was the Treasurer of the Chamber. Henry chose his Treasurers ... for their competence. Their impressive performance may have had something to do with the attention this accountant-on-the-throne paid to their work, signing each page of their accounts with the royal monogram once their arithmetic had been approved.[2]

Under Henry VII's most illustrious Tudor successors, Henry VIII and Elizabeth I, the monarch became more detached from the details of administration, and the politician/bureaucrat hybrid developed apace. Thomas Wolsey, Thomas Cromwell and William Cecil (Lord Burghley) were key figures in sixteenth century government. Cromwell, especially, accumulated an array of offices, and supervised the creation of a new departmental structure, Privy Council, and associated institutions.

Among the important institutional developments of the seventeenth century were the formation of the Committee of Trade (spawned by the Privy Council in 1621), and the rise of the Treasury in the wake of the Restoration. The man who served as Secretary to the five Treasury Commissioners, Sir George Downing, will forever be associated with the narrow street he built off Whitehall, but his administrative impact was of greater significance than his talent for construction. Under this former spy, who renounced his allegiance to Oliver Cromwell just in time to find a place in the government of Charles II, the Treasury asserted its power over all matters relating to revenue, and began to use imported modern methods of accounting and control.

By the middle of the eighteenth century, even before the advent of income tax (this came during the Napoleonic Wars), some 80 per cent of all people employed in government were involved in revenue-raising. The Treasury had already carved out a leading role for itself when, in 1782, George III and his Prime Minister, Rockingham, transformed the Northern and Southern Departments of the Office of the Principal Secretary of State into two new Whitehall departments, the Home Office and the Foreign Office.

During the same decade, the first serious attack on the inefficiencies of the civil service was made by the MP and political philosopher, Edmund Burke. His 1780 speech on the need for 'economical reform', especially in the Privy Council's Committee (or 'Board') of Trade, led to the abolition of the latter two years later. A reformed Board of Trade was established in 1786, under two ministers and a small staff of officials.

This distinction between government ministers on the one hand, and subordinate officials on the other, emerged during the late eighteenth and early nineteenth centuries. The bureaucrat-cum-politician (typified by Thomas Cromwell in the sixteenth century) was superseded by the distinct breeds of ministers and civil servants, partly because of a division of labour brought about by increasingly heavy workloads. The common origins of the two breeds are betrayed by job titles, especially by the use of the ubiquitous 'secretary' (Secretary of State and Under Secretary on the political side, Permanent Secretary and Deputy Secretary on the official side, for instance). Another contributing factor to this distinction was the entrenchment of the convention of government and opposition, with one ministerial team departing *en bloc* when it had lost the confidence of king and/or Parliament. In this climate, it was recognised that most government posts would not change hands on a change of government. Posts below the rank of minister were viewed, in legal terms, as the property of the office-holder. The system of patronage allowed politicians to find secure jobs (sometimes sinecures – posts with no real duties) for friends and acquaintances. The concept of a permanent civil service, albeit flavoured with patronage and corruption, was taking root.

By the beginning of the nineteenth century there were some limited signs that the concept of a cohesive 'civil service' was emerging to challenge the traditional, non-corporate, departmental basis of the public service. One illustration of this trend was the establishment, in 1810, of a pension scheme for civil servants across the range of government departments, under the watchful eye of the Treasury. It would be wrong to place too much emphasis on this type of development, nonetheless, since the Victorian civil service remained in essence a collection of disparate departments, and the idea of a unified civil service was as yet inchoate.

2. Emergence of the modern civil service

The administrative historian Henry Parris has commented:

> The 'permanent civil service' prior to [1780] differed from its modern counterpart in three significant ways. It was not permanent, it was not civil, and it was not a service. . . .[3]

As we have seen, by the early part of the nineteenth century it was possible to discern two of the characteristics Parris associated with a modern permanent civil service: permanency in the face of changes of government, and a reasonably distinctive civil, non-political role.

In the course of the century the British administrative machine was to develop some of the key features of a 'service', as defined by Parris. A start had been made with the introduction of uniform rules on pensions, already alluded to. Before the end of the Victorian period a significant leap forward towards the creation of a modern civil service would be taken through the advent of new systems of recruitment and conditions of service.

To a significant extent, this was a consequence of the remarkable growth in the scale and activity of government during the nineteenth century. As government intervention in social and economic matters increased, even in the face of the prevailing doctrine of *laissez-faire*, so the civil service expanded. In 1815 over 24,500 people were employed in central government departments. Although the number fell to under 17,000 in the early 1840s, and was subject to occasional fluctuations, the general trend was upwards, and by the 1890s Britain had some 80,000 civil servants. In the light of this expansion, critics perceived inherited institutions and methods to be of decreasing utility. A number of parliamentary inquiries were mounted into the efficiency of government departments. In 1848 the most important of these was launched by the Commons Select Committee on Miscellaneous Expenditure. This committee took evidence from, among others, Charles Trevelyan.

Educated at the East India Company's Haileybury College, Trevelyan worked in the Indian Civil Service (where, at the age of twenty-one, he had his superior dismissed for bribery), and married the sister of the prominent historian/politician Thomas Babington (later Lord) Macaulay, before being appointed to the top civil service post (then Assistant Secretary, in modern terms Permanent Secretary) at the Treasury when only thirty-two years old. After initiating a series of reforms in the Treasury, Trevelyan began to argue for a fundamental reform of the civil service as a whole.

He failed to convince the Commons committee of the merits of his proposals for recruitment to the civil service by means of competitive examination, and a division of departmental work into 'mechanical' and 'intellectual' tasks. However, during the next few years he did succeed in influencing the outcomes of economy reviews in a number of Whitehall departments. The new ideas were resented and bitterly opposed in some quarters, especially in the bastions of civil service conservatism, the Home Office and the Foreign Office. It was Trevelyan's good fortune that Gladstone was appointed as Chancellor of the Exchequer, and thus his new political boss, in 1852. Gladstone had considerable sympathy with his senior official's ideas, and encouraged him to continue the departmental reviews. Furthermore, in the spring of 1853 the Chancellor launched a Whitehall-wide investigation, to be headed by Trevelyan and Sir Stafford Northcote, one of Gladstone's political protégés. The result of this investigation, the Northcote-Trevelyan Report,[4] was published in February 1854.

In summary form, the Report recommended the division of civil service posts into those dealing with 'mechanical' and those dealing with 'intellectual' tasks, recruitment to the service by open competitive examination supervised by a Civil Service Board, promotion within the service on the basis of merit, and inter-departmental transfers of staff in order to facilitate a more homogeneous service.

> The completed report was a charter for meritocracy – the determined recruitment of talent, its promotion on the basis of demonstrable merit and its efficient distribution throughout the public service to rid Whitehall of patronage, inefficiency and narrow departmentalism in one go.[5]

Defenders of the existing order, from Queen Victoria and some senior Cabinet ministers downwards, saw the Northcote-Trevelyan Report as an unwelcome manifesto for the virtues of 'merit' and 'talent' at the expense of those of 'solid character' and 'breeding'. The argument put forward by one George Arbuthnot in favour of the traditional civil service was typical:

> In order to direct details effectively, an officer ought to know how to do them himself. In order to become acquainted with technical or legal phraseology, the young clerk must begin by copying documents. As in professional pursuits, the efficient Civil Servant is formed by making him in the first instance a good workman. The most distinguished officers of this class commenced early in life at the drudgery of the desk.[6]

Recruitment and promotion on merit would have destroyed this concept of a long civil service apprenticeship, and, Arbuthnot might have added, ended opportunities for patronage and jobbery.

The forces of conservatism succeeded in blocking any immediate move towards implementing Northcote-Trevelyan. However, a combination of factors came to the aid of the reformers. Among these were:

1 the scandalous revelations regarding the organisation of supplies for the British forces fighting in the Crimean War, which created new doubts about the British administrative machine;

2 the emergence of the vigorous Administrative Reform Association, a broadly based organisation containing such luminaries as Charles Dickens, which lobbied for a range of governmental reforms, and gave added impetus to the spirit of Northcote-Trevelyan;

3 the obvious success of Trevelyan's brother-in-law, Macaulay, in sponsoring a reorganisation of the Indian Civil Service demonstrated the potential of reform;

4 the weight thrown behind the Northcote-Trevelyan scheme by educational reformers such as Jowett of Balliol College, Oxford and Vaughan, Headmaster of Harrow, who could see the opportunities which would open up for graduates in a reformed civil service, offered a prestigious counter-balance to the negative attitude which was to be found elsewhere in the 'establishment'.

As a result, a partial and piecemeal implementation of the Northcote-Trevelyan recommendations was set in motion. A three-man Civil Service Commission was set up in 1855, and although this body was but a diluted version of the Board envisaged by Northcote and Trevelyan, it did have the power to issue 'certificates of fitness' to candidates for recruitment to the service. Nonetheless, the examination competitions sponsored by the Commission were, in many cases, distinctly bogus, with 'idiot' candidates being put up against a minister's nominee, merely to give the appearance of a 'competition'. Ministerial nomination continued to be the most common means of entry to the civil service for some time to come.

A more significant change came in 1870, with Gladstone now Prime Minister, and another dedicated reformer, Robert Lowe, as Chancellor of the Exchequer. The Civil Service Order in Council of 4 June 1870 ensured that the Commission would oversee a system of genuine competitive examination in all departments (with the temporary exceptions of the Home Office and the Foreign Office, whose ministers vetoed the new arrangements). The examination system was specifically designed to cater for two types of candidate: those for the higher posts with 'intellectual' tasks, and those for the lower posts with 'mechanical' tasks.

Limited steps towards greater unification within the civil service were recommended by the Playfair Report in 1875, which endorsed inter-departmental staff transfers and a reform of the grading structure. The same themes formed the basis of the Ridley Report in 1886.

As the twentieth century dawned, the civil service was beginning to assume some of the key characteristics favoured by Northcote and Trevelyan. Their ideal was far short of complete realisation nonetheless. Many political and official heads of departments held serious reservations about the competitive entry system, and departmentalism remained a dominant feature in Whitehall. Each department of state cherished its history, traditions, image, forms of organisation and modes of operation.

The Northcote-Trevelyan prescription for change was entirely appropriate for its time, the latter part of the nineteenth century. The partial and piecemeal method of implementation ensured, however, that the scale and responsibilities of government had increased significantly to overtake the assumptions of Northcote and Trevelyan before their ideas were accepted in most corners of Whitehall. By the time the radicalism of Northcote-Trevelyan had become the orthodox creed, the administrative agenda had been rewritten. It is the remarkable growth in government, and its impact on the civil service, to which we will now turn.

3. Impact of welfare and war, 1905–19

It would be a crude oversimplification to suggest that the end of the Victorian period marked a definitive watershed between strict *laissez-faire*, non-interventionist government and large-scale government involvement in every area of life. In fact, numerous and accumulating examples of government intervention in social and economic affairs were to be seen in the course of the nineteenth century. Furthermore, even in the twentieth century, the concept of intervention was to have its limits. Nonetheless, the early years of the new century witnessed a major shift away from the minimalist, 'nightwatchman' state, towards a more positive conception of the role of government.

Few contemporary commentators would have predicted that the Liberal administration which took office under the ageing Campbell-Bannerman in December 1905 would leave its mark as one of the two great reforming governments of the twentieth century. The Liberals unexpectedly won a landslide victory in the January 1906 General Election, and by the time they moved into a coalition in circumstances of war in 1915, they had secured the passage of a series of reforms which brought significant new responsibilities to the civil service machine. The keystones of the reform programme were set in place under Campbell-Bannerman's successor from 1908, Asquith. His ministry of all the talents established a precedent for government intervention in industrial disputes, widened and improved the system of inspection of factories, introduced a nationwide system of labour exchanges, and initiated the old age pension and national insurance schemes. The major reforms were pioneered by Asquith himself, Lloyd George at the Board of Trade and the Treasury, and Churchill at the Board of Trade and the Home Office. The civil service grew apace in this atmosphere. In 1901, there had been around 116,000 civil servants in Britain. By 1914 there were over 282,000.

The administrative machine was facing up to its new tasks at precisely the time when the competitive entry system was beginning to have an impact on the top civil service posts. The successful candidates in the new examination were working their way up the hierarchy. Still, many senior posts continued to be filled by ministerial patronage or through direct recruitment. The consequences of this were not invariably negative:

> The first career Home Office official to become permanent under secretary in that department was not appointed until 1908. . . . Many of the principal officials of the Board of Trade before 1914 had also not entered the civil service straight from university or through competitive examinations. Its eminent permanent secretary from 1907 to 1919, Sir Hubert Llewellyn Smith, had originally been recruited in 1893 following his work as a lecturer and researcher. William Beveridge was appointed by Winston Churchill in 1908 as an outside expert. . . . In the period 1900–1919, 14 out of a total of 47 permanent secretaries (29.8 per cent) had entered the civil service from other types of work. . . . [7]

The 'cult' of the general administrator, able to turn his hand to the work of any Whitehall department, had yet to become entrenched, and special skills or expertise could still secure a senior appointment.

The embryonic welfare state ushered in by the Liberal reforms brought new challenges for the civil service. Even more were on the way. The pressure of war was to stretch the capacity of the government machine to its limit, and effectively force through a series of structural and organisational changes, some of which would become entrenched. At the forefront of this process was the dynamic personality of David Lloyd George. Chancellor of the Exchequer at the outbreak of hostilities in 1914, he became Minister of Munitions on the formation of the coalition in May 1915, before ousting Asquith and becoming Prime Minister in a new coalition in December 1916.

As Chancellor, he took upon himself the task of enforcing the Defence of the Realm Act, which gave the government sweeping powers to intervene in industrial and social affairs, in the interest of the war effort. As Minister of Munitions he built from scratch a new super-department of 25,000 civil servants (some recruited directly, some seconded from other departments) which established a war economy. By the end of 1916 he was in a position to turn his attention to the heart of the machinery of government, the Cabinet system itself. Lloyd George had been frustrated by what he saw as the inefficiencies of the Asquith Cabinet. He immediately dispensed with the full, 22-member Cabinet and introduced a new body, modelled on the hitherto unofficial 'War Committee' and the pre-war Committee of Imperial Defence. Lloyd George's War Cabinet was to have only five members, would work to a formal agenda and have its minutes recorded. The administrative support for this new body would be provided by a Cabinet Office, headed by Maurice Hankey, who was soon designated Cabinet Secretary. The minutes of a British Cabinet meeting were first taken on 9 December 1916, and from that day the decision-making process came to be centred on the flow of documents from the Cabinet.

In addition to the Cabinet Office, Lloyd George created his own Prime Minister's Secretariat, the so-called 'Garden Suburb' based in some huts to the rear of Number 10 Downing Street. Until its abolition in 1918, this brought together civil servants and 'outsiders' in a team of advisers whose fundamental purpose was to allow the

Prime Minister to keep in touch with developments throughout the rapidly expanding Whitehall village.

Whitehall was expanding, both in terms of the sheer number of officials working there, and in terms of departmental multiplication. In 1917 Lloyd George set up a new Air Ministry, Ministry of Labour, Department of National Service, Ministry of Shipping, Ministry of Food and Ministry of Reconstruction. Career civil servants were working alongside temporary 'irregulars' in these 'mushroom ministries'. Despite complaints from some senior figures, concerned about the impact of the newcomers on traditional civil service values, the result was positive enough from the government's point of view:

> wartime Whitehall was acquiring at last the kind of planning and executive machinery for manpower, production and distribution that it had needed since the armies of the Central Powers mobilised in July and August 1914.[8]

In the midst of the hubbub of activity which was Whitehall at war, some thought was being given to the requirements of the post-war government. The last major investigation into the civil service had turned out to be a somewhat anaemic affair, the MacDonnell Royal Commission of 1912–14. One constructive proposal which emerged from this Commission related to the central management of the civil service. MacDonnell recommended the creation of a special section, located within the Treasury, to oversee this function. The desirability of having a central management capability, particularly in the light of the rapid expansion of the service, was recognised by the Haldane Report of 1918.[9] R. B. Haldane's Machinery of Government Committee was a 1917 offshoot from the Reconstruction Committee (later Ministry) of the Lloyd George coalition. Haldane had been a senior figure in the pre-war Liberal government, and he came to share Lloyd George's distaste for the mode of operation of that government. Not surprisingly, therefore, the Report found favour with, and effectively sanctified, many of the war-time developments, especially the new Cabinet system. Haldane proposed further reforms, including the permanent use of a small Cabinet, the creation of a central research capability to facilitate medium-term and long-term policy planning, and a rationalisation of departmental responsibilities.

In many respects, Haldane and his colleagues on the Committee were farsighted.[10] However, in the event, most of the Report's recommendations were to be ignored. The dominant desire in post-war Whitehall was to be for a measure of consolidation, and a 'return to normalcy' wherever possible. Of course, the clock could not be turned back to 1914, and the machinery of government after the First World War would inevitably bear many of the imprints of that extraordinary period.

4. Fisher at the helm, 1919–39

In a period of just under one year, from the summer of 1919 to the summer of 1920, there took place a series of developments which were to cast the mould for the inter-war civil service.

- On 5 August 1919 the Cabinet Committee on Finance approved the recommendation of an internal Treasury inquiry headed by Sir John Bradbury (one of three joint Permanent Secretaries at the Treasury). Bradbury's report resulted in a restructuring of the Treasury along functional lines, with one branch ('Establishments') dealing with civil service organisation, manpower and pay.
- On 15 September 1919 a Treasury circular stated that the Permanent Secretary to the Treasury was to become 'Permanent Head of the Civil Service' and would advise the Prime Minister on civil service appointments and honours.
- On 1 October 1919 Sir Warren Fisher became Permanent Secretary to the Treasury. The wartime system of three, co-equal joint Permanent Secretaries was gradually dismantled in the period leading up to Fisher's appointment.
- On 12 March 1920 a Treasury circular implemented a Cabinet decision that the consent of the Prime Minister would be required for the appointment or removal of Permanent Secretaries and other senior officials in all departments. This was a blow against departmentalism and a step towards greater unification of the service.
- On 22 July 1920 an Order in Council formally conferred upon the Treasury power over all civil service management and personnel issues.

The leading role of the Treasury, which had been a fact since the earliest days of the British 'civil service', was thus reasserted and strengthened in the wake of a period of extraordinary upheaval in Whitehall. What had previously been left to 'convention' and 'understanding' was now formulated in specific documents. The man charged with the task of fulfilling this role, the new Permanent Secretary to the Treasury and Head of the Civil Service, was only thirty-nine years old. Sir Warren Fisher would retain his place at the top of the Whitehall hierarchy for the next twenty years. During that time there would be five different Prime Ministers and nine different governments (ten if we consider MacDonald's first National Government of August to November 1931 separately). Power would alternate between coalitions of various hues, the Labour Party and the Conservative Party. Through it all, Fisher remained at his desk. The only other civil servant who could match this record of continuous service in a very senior post was the Cabinet Secretary Sir Maurice Hankey (1916–38). However, he had been put in his place by Fisher at a fairly early stage when he was reminded that he was a 'Secretary' and should not be tempted to formulate vague Cabinet discussions into minutes which gave precise policy guidance.[11]

It is difficult to avoid recording a negative verdict on Fisher's custodianship of the civil service. This is not to deny him credit for some important achievements. By using the Treasury circulars and Order in Council of 1919–20 he succeeded in imposing a greater degree of unity than the departments in Whitehall had ever seen. Inter-departmental staff transfers became the norm and officials began to view the service as a corporate entity. Fisher denied the Treasury the opportunity to select the cream of the recruits from the entrance examinations by requiring all Treasury officials to have previous experience in other departments. A further spur towards greater cohesion, though one which was less welcome to Fisher, was the emergence of trade unionism on a service-wide basis. The small Whitehall unions which had been developing since the late nineteenth century were given formal bargaining rights in the management–union Whitley Councils, set up in 1919. Fisher adopted a relatively high profile as Head of the Civil Service, even in what seem rather minor matters such as the creation of sporting and social clubs. Arguably, he overemphasised this role at the expense of his duties as Permanent Secretary to the Treasury: Winston Churchill, Chancellor of the

Exchequer, complained in 1926 that he had not seen Fisher for 18 months![12]

There was, however, a fatal flaw in Fisher's approach which ensured that, despite increasing corporate cohesion and mobility between departments, the civil service of 1939 was in danger of stagnating. He adhered rather too rigidly to the Northcote-Trevelyan prescription, though it was seventy, then eighty years out of date:

A major feature of the Fisher era was the emergence of the 'generalist' as the ideal-type top-level administrator in Whitehall ... there was a reduction in the number of senior officials with work experience outside government service: in the 1920–44 period, for instance, 8 out of a total of 62 (12.7 per cent) permanent secretaries had some outside experience before entering Whitehall (compared with 29.8 per cent in the previous years 1900–1919)).[13]

In his evidence to the Tomlin Royal Commission on the Civil Service in 1930 Fisher made clear his opinion that the senior posts in Whitehall should preferably be circulated between a tight corps of generalists. People with specialised knowledge and expertise had their place, but it was not at the top of the hierarchy.

One serious result of Fisher's rather rigid approach was that

By the late 1930s the Civil Service was a staid organisation at virtually every level ... a service in which the clerks were drawn from the secondary schools, the executive officers from the grammar school sixth forms and the administrators from the universities – careers for life with precious little movement from grade to grade ... orthodoxy and hierarchy became entrenched in Warren Fisher's Whitehall – with the expert caged and the generalist roaming free ....[14]

Towards the end of his long period at the helm, Fisher encountered a Prime Minister, Neville Chamberlain, who interpreted the power of Downing Street over senior civil service appointments in a more assertive fashion than that to which the Head of the Civil Service was accustomed. In January 1938 the Permanent Secretary at the Foreign Office, Sir Robert Vansittart (Fisher's candidate for that post in 1930) was moved into an essentially meaningless post as 'Chief Diplomatic Adviser' in order to accommodate

Figure 2.1: Top civil service posts since the Second World War

Permanent Secretary to the Treasury

Warren Fisher, 1919–39
Richard Hopkins, 1939–45
Edward Bridges, 1945–56
Norman Brook (joint), 1956–62
Roger Makins (joint), 1956–60
Frank Lee (joint), 1960–62
William Armstrong (joint), 1962–68
Laurence Helsby (joint), 1963–68
Douglas Allen, 1968–74
Douglas Wass, 1974–83
Peter Middleton, 1983–91
Terry Burns, 1991–

Cabinet Secretary

Maurice Hankey, 1916–38
Edward Bridges, 1938–47
Norman Brook, 1947–62
Burke Trend, 1962–73
John Hunt, 1973–79
Robert Armstrong, 1979–88
Robin Butler, 1988–

Head of the Civil Service

Warren Fisher, 1919–39
Horace Wilson, 1939–42
Richard Hopkins, 1942–45
Edward Bridges, 1945–56
Norman Brook, 1956–63
Laurence Helsby, 1963–68
William Armstrong, 1968–74
Douglas Allen, 1974–78
Ian Bancroft, 1978–81
Douglas Wass (joint), 1981–83
Robert Armstrong (joint), 1981–83
Robert Armstrong, 1983–88
Robin Butler, 1988–

Chamberlain's choice, Sir Alexander Cadogan. The moving force
behind this appointment was Sir Horace Wilson, formally the
government's 'Chief Industrial Adviser', but with an active role in
the creation of Chamberlain's foreign policy. There is a certain
irony in the fact that Fisher, who had striven to eliminate systematic
political influence over civil service appointments, was succeeded
at the Treasury and as Head of the Civil Service by Sir Horace
Wilson in 1939.

5. 'Hitler's reforms': Impact of the Second World War

Peter Hennessy has dubbed the effect of the Second World War on
the British civil service 'Hitler's Reform'.[15] An influx of new
people combined with the adoption of different modes of operation
to shake Whitehall out of the torpor into which it had been sliding
in the 1930s.

In the latter part of that decade, the worsening international
climate led Hankey and Fisher to draft, and periodically update,
blueprints for a reshaping of the government machine in circumstances of war. Their basic model was the Whitehall of 1918.
Whatever criticisms may be levelled at Britain's relative lack of
military preparedness in September 1939, it should be acknowledged
that the administrative machine was ready to switch into a war
mode almost immediately.

A Central Register contained the names of people whose
academic, technical or professional backgrounds could be of use in
the higher reaches of the civil service, and this was activated on the
outbreak of hostilities. 'Irregular', temporary civil servants were
recruited into the existing Whitehall departments and a new set of
'mushroom ministries' (such as Food, Supply, Economic Warfare,
Information, and Fuel and Power). Scientists, industrialists and
social scientists of all descriptions were summoned into a special
form of national service.

A small army of officials was required to run the central and
regional boards on which employers and trade unions were represented, and which were designed to achieve the maximum
amount of cooperation in the war industries. To an even more
marked degree than during the First World War, Britain became a
command economy, with massive state intervention in the supply
of basic foodstuffs and clothing to the people, and raw materials to

industry. In all, the numbers of civil servants leapt from 374,000 in 1939 to 667,000 by 1945. In these circumstances, rigid distinctions between civil service grades, and between 'generalists' and 'specialists', began to break down.

One illustration of the new fluidity is the remarkable experience of Oliver (later Lord) Franks. As a university Professor of Moral Philosophy he had signed a piece of paper in 1938 agreeing to go wherever he was sent in the event of a national emergency. He was sent to the Ministry of Supply in September 1939, moved through the civil service grades at an astonishing pace, and became 'the public servant who wielded the greatest ever powers over British industry'.[16]

The two most significant temporary civil servants in Whitehall were John Maynard Keynes and William Beveridge. For each of these academics, this was the third period of temporary work in the civil service (the others had come under the Asquith Government and during the First World War). Keynes carved a role for himself as an adviser to the Treasury, and played a major part in shaping Britain's economic strategy for the peace. Beveridge started off in the Ministry of Labour, where he so irritated his minister, Ernest Bevin, that he was shunted into the chairmanship of a committee inquiring into social insurance. He drove this committee to exceed its terms of reference (would a career civil servant have done this?) and in 1942 it produced what would become one of the keystones of the post-war social order, the Beveridge Report.

While the irregulars were making their mark in the upper reaches of Whitehall, some senior officials made the leap between 'administration' and 'policy'. Among the civil servants who left officialdom to move into ministerial posts were Sir Maurice Hankey (the former Cabinet Secretary who was in turn, Minister Without Portfolio, Chancellor of the Duchy of Lancaster, and Paymaster General between 1938 and 1942), Sir James Grigg (Permanent Secretary at the War Office who served as Secretary of State for War, 1942–45) and Sir John Anderson (former Permanent Secretary at the Ministry of Shipping and then the Home Office, who during the war was a senior minister in a series of posts, including the Home Secretaryship and the Chancellorship). Among his other duties, Anderson chaired a Cabinet committee which conducted a running inquiry into the machinery of government.

On becoming Prime Minister in May 1940, Winston Churchill chose to utilise a small War Cabinet, as had David Lloyd George during the First World War. This necessitated a strong underpinning of Cabinet committees, to handle most aspects of domestic policy and the details of military planning. Sir Edward Bridges, Cabinet Secretary since 1938, naturally had a key coordinating role in relation to these committees. Indeed, his biographer argues that Bridges made a vital contribution to the successful conduct of government during the war:

> Under Bridges as Secretary, the Offices of the War Cabinet became the nerve centre of the war effort, manned day and night .... Although he had no executive responsibilities outside his own office he undoubtedly had an immensely important position in the government machine. Bridges was always being consulted by those making or contributing to decisions .... He regarded it as one of his main functions to ensure that, before any decisions were taken, all the relevant facts had been assembled and the right people consulted.[17]

During the last few months of the war Bridges combined the post of Permanent Secretary to the Treasury and Head of the Civil Service with that of Cabinet Secretary. 'Head of the Civil Service' by now referred only to the home civil service, as the Foreign Office officials and the diplomatic corps had formally been separated from the home departments in 1943. As the war ended, Bridges relinquished the Cabinet Secretaryship in order to concentrate on his new role.

6. Managing the Welfare State, 1945–79

Some of the social reforms instituted by the Liberal Government in the early years of the twentieth century were developed, in piecemeal fashion, during the decades which followed. However, it was not until the period of Labour Government between 1945 and 1951 that a coordinated and detailed legislative package was devised, with the explicit intention of creating a new social and economic order. By the time the Attlee Government fell from power in 1951, a National Health Service had been established, the system of national insurance had been expanded to cover virtually the entire population, and wartime control of key industries had been extended through the device of nationalisation. Supervisory powers over the new public corporations were vested in Whitehall departments.

The work of the Attlee Government set the agenda for the next thirty years. Conservative governments (1951–64 and 1970–74) and Labour governments (1964–70 and 1974–79) set about administering a 'mixed economy' and 'welfare state'. The precise location of the boundary between the public and private sector was a subject for occasional, bitter party disputes. However, the principle of state control in key industries and services, within the framework of a capitalist system, was accepted by both parties in government. The maintenance of 'full' employment, secured by utilising Keynesian economic management techniques, was also accepted as a basic objective. Similarly, Labour and Conservative governments were both committed to an expanded system of social security benefits and national health care.

The civil service would be called upon to operate and oversee this expanding range of state commitments. As the temporary, wartime civil servants departed from Whitehall (with a few exceptions), the new Head of the Civil Service, Sir Edward Bridges, blocked any fundamental inquiry into its mode of operation. Perhaps surprisingly in view of the success of the civil service 'irregulars' between 1939 and 1945, Bridges assumed the mantle of Fisher, and vigorously defended the attributes of the generalist administrator. In this task, Bridges was ably assisted by another traditionalist who had been schooled in the inter-war civil service, Norman Brook. He was Secretary to the Cabinet between 1947 and 1962, and took on the posts of Permanent Secretary to the Treasury and Head of the Civil Service following Bridges' retirement in 1956. A Bridges-Brook axis dominated the running of the civil service in much the same way as a Fisher-Hankey axis had operated between the wars. Bridges and Brook can take some credit for securing the entrenchment of the system of· standing Cabinet committees, which had been used to relieve the War and Attlee Cabinets of much detailed business.

The organisation over which Bridges and Brook presided was being stretched to the limit of its capacity by the challenges facing post-war governments. Stresses and strains were becoming apparent. The 'man in Whitehall' had never been the most likeable figure in British popular mythology, but in the early 1950s the concept of the unyielding bureaucrat took on a new force. Impatience at continuing shortages some six and seven years after the end of war undoubtedly played a part in this. In this light, perhaps it is not entirely surprising that the initial interpretations of the resignation of the Agriculture Minister, Sir Thomas Dugdale, in 1954, placed the politician in the role of sacrificial lamb, taking upon himself the blame for errors committed by his inflexible officials. Indeed, the official inquiry into what came to be known as the Crichel Down affair actually named and blamed the civil servants.[18] In fact, it now seems clear that Dugdale was the victim of his political opponents in the Conservative Party rather than the fall-guy for bureaucratic bunglers, but that was not how the affair was initially presented.[19]

As the decade progressed, the civil service began to be allocated its share of the blame for Britain's relative economic decline and loss of international standing.[20] The 1960s were years when a number of attempts were made to fine-tune the machinery of government, especially its economic components. The Plowden Report of 1961 led to the establishment of the PESC (Public Expenditure Survey Committee) system, which was designed to facilitate more coherent economic planning and expenditure control. The Treasury was partially restructured as a consequence.

More significant restructuring came with the return of a Labour Government, under Harold Wilson, in 1964. A new Department of Economic Affairs was set up, with George Brown as its ministerial chief. The DEA was specifically designed to counter the power and influence of the Treasury. The failure of Brown's 'National Plan' (blown off course by persistent sterling and balance of payments crises) followed by his departure for the Foreign Office, left the DEA exposed, and its demise in 1969 came as no surprise.

The DEA's lack of impact, Britain's continuing economic stagnation, and a vogue for institutional soul-searching led to serious questions being asked about the operation of the machinery of government in this period. In 1966 an inquiry was launched into the structure, recruitment and management of the civil service. It was chaired by a former wartime 'irregular', the Vice-Chancellor of Sussex University, Lord Fulton.

The Fulton Report, published in 1968,[21] sparked off a wide-ranging debate on the civil service. The general tone of the report was set by its assertion that:

> The Home Civil Service today is still fundamentally the product of the nineteenth-century philosophy of the Northcote-Trevelyan Report. The problems it faces are those of the second half of the twentieth century. In spite of its many strengths, it is inadequate ... for the most efficient discharge of the present and prospective responsibilities of government ....

Fulton made 158 recommendations. Among other things, the report argued for a break with the 'cult of the generalist', the opening up of opportunities for specialists through ending the highly stratified system of career paths, encouragement of a greater concern for management through the establishment of a new Civil Service Department, and a major review of methods of recruitment.

The criticisms contained in the document ensured that it had a mixed reception, at best, in the Whitehall corridors. Fulton's description of general administrators as 'amateurs' and the accusation that the civil service had not fundamentally changed in over a century rankled with the most senior civil servants, the so-called 'mandarins', and many of their subordinates.

In spite of its endorsement by the Prime Minister and the Leader of the Opposition, the letter of Fulton was only partially introduced, and the spirit hardly at all. The Civil Service Department was set up, an inquiry was launched into recruitment (this recommended a widening of the main recruitment grounds for Administration Trainees, the potential high-flyers, beyond Oxbridge), a Civil Service College was established to provide management training, and a unified pay and grading system (the 'Open Structure') was created for officials ranked Under Secretary and above (this was subsequently extended, see Figure 1.1). However, one of Fulton's main thrusts was thwarted. The proposed integration of specialists and general administrators throughout the service was circumvented, partly through determined manoeuvring on the part of senior officials, especially Sir William Armstrong, Head of the Civil Service. Armstrong got around the desire of the Prime Minister, Harold Wilson, to see unified grades for specialists and generalists:

> ... his (Armstrong's) idea of Government policy was not that
> unified grading was practicable and would be carried out; but
> that unified grading would only occur if it was deemed
> practicable.[22]

One of the characteristics of the late 1960s machinery of government which caused Fulton some concern was the growing size and
complexity of departments, and the consequences of this for
effective management. Departmental 'giantism' could be seen in
the amalgamation of the Admiralty, the War Office and the Air
Ministry into the Ministry of Defence in 1964, and the unification
of the Foreign and Commonwealth Offices in 1968. Perhaps the
clearest manifestation of this phenomenon was the creation of the
Department of Health and Social Security in 1968. By the early
1970s the DHSS had a staff of over 70,000, and a decade later
some 95,000 civil servants, ranging from Administrative Assistants
in the benefit offices to the Permanent Secretary in his office suite,
were employed in this pillar of the welfare state.

The Conservative Government of Edward Heath in the early
1970s adopted the concept of super-departments with some
enthusiasm. The Ministry of Housing and Local Government was
merged with the Ministry of Public Building and Works to form
the Department of the Environment, the Departments of Trade
and Industry were amalgamated. The organisational principles of
'giantism' could be criticised on a number of grounds, but one of
the weaknesses inherent in a super-department was the blurring of
the respective role responsibilities of ministers and their senior
officials. This was most clearly illustrated during the Vehicle and
General affair, which was in some senses the 'Crichel Down
revisited' of the early 1970s. The collapse of this insurance company,
with one million policy-holders, was blamed on an Under Secretary
in the Department of Trade and Industry, while his civil service
superiors and his Secretary of State were exonerated.[23]

During the 1970s, the civil service came to resemble an institution
under siege. Critics on the left and right alike seemed to agree on
one thing at least: the civil service was 'too powerful'. It was
accused of defusing and neutralising the Fulton reforms, blowing
governments of both parties off their radical courses and back
towards a cosy consensus, and wasting public funds through massive

inefficiency and sheer profligacy. The army of bureaucrats (747,000 strong in 1975, including the industrial civil servants) with inflation-proof pensions (introduced in 1971) became easy targets in an era of rapidly rising prices.

It was perhaps inevitable that the burden of such criticisms would take its toll, coming as they did at a time when the service was being asked to run a welfare state in the face of severe economic crises. The mental collapse of Sir William Armstrong, Head of the Civil Service, in February 1974 could be seen as a symbol for the entire service in that decade. It did not collapse, of course, but as it rumbled towards the 1980s this part of the machinery of government seemed to be desperately in need of an overhaul. When it came, it seemed to many in Whitehall as if the overhaul was being carried out by apprentice mechanics who had little respect for the old machine.

7. 'De-privileged' and streamlined? Towards the next century

The remaining chapters of this book are largely concerned with the civil service post-1979. At this point, it will be sufficient to establish some of the main themes of this period.

Margaret Thatcher came to power pledged to reform many aspects of the British polity. The civil service did not escape her attention. In her words, it was to be 'de-privileged', knocked off its high pedestal. The new Conservative Government launched an attack on the post-war 'consensus'. It is fair to say that the principles which underpinned the welfare state and the mixed economy had been under question since the mid-1970s, at the latest, but it was to be the Thatcher Government which overtly challenged the post-1945 economic and social order.

The managers of this order, the civil servants, were to be reduced in number (to fewer than 570,000 by 1989). The influence of the most senior officials was to be diluted somewhat, with the Prime Minister in particular inclining towards alternative sources of advice. At the same time, partly through sheer good fortune, Thatcher was to be given an unprecedented opportunity to make a large number of appointments to the top posts in the civil service, promoting those who shared her basic outlook. A fresh dose of 'managerialism' was to be injected into Whitehall and its outposts, with the predominant concern being 'value for money'. As far as accountability and openness were concerned, there were conflicting signs. In one respect, the civil service was opened up to a more sustained and regular degree of scrutiny than ever before, with officials being called before Commons select committees on a more systematic basis. In other senses the hatches of secrecy were battened down very firmly, with apparently unending searches for Whitehall 'moles' and a series of highly publicised prosecutions.

Despite this cascade of changes, the extent to which the Thatcher Government succeeded in fundamentally transforming the civil service remains a moot point. To what extent were the key characteristics which emerged from the process of historical evolution ('permanency', 'neutrality', and 'anonymity') altered or abandoned in the period after 1979?

It is to this, and other themes, that we must now switch our attention.

3 Civil Servants and Ministers

The relationship between departmental civil servants and their ministerial chiefs has often attracted academic attention. In part, this is because the relationship epitomises the complex interaction of political and official structures, without which the British constitution is inexplicable. During recent years many of the assumptions and understandings surrounding the working environment of government ministers and their officials have changed under the pressure of political events.

This chapter explores the relationship between ministers and the civil service with reference to a number of key themes. We look first at the doctrine of individual ministerial responsibility, since this establishes the broad framework within which all ministers and civil servants operate. Then the various roles of departmental officials are examined. Working relationships are considered through case studies and, finally, the central issue of policy is raised, together with the ambiguous role of the civil service in this sphere.

The doctrine of individual ministerial responsibility
Individual ministerial responsibility, one of the central tenets of the British constitution, is also one of the most misunderstood constitutional devices. If the doctrine means anything, it is often argued, ministers ought to resign when major failings occur in the realm of their departmental responsibilities. Since this never happens, the doctrine is meaningless! Alternatively, it is argued that occasional, well-publicised ministerial resignations prove beyond doubt that individual ministerial responsibility is alive and well, or has recently been 'revived' after a long period of slumber.

To equate the doctrine with resignations in this way is misleading, simplistic and unproductive. The so-called 'resignation clause' (or, in our terms, the sanctions element) of the doctrine is by no means its most significant aspect. Individual ministerial responsibility serves to establish the framework for the complex relationships between government ministers and Parliament and, crucially, between ministers and their own departmental civil servants. It defines the scope and nature of the powers vested in these ministers. The doctrine lies at the very heart of the British constitution; without a clear understanding of its working and implications, one cannot hope to comprehend the relationship between civil servants and ministers. One way to approach a closer understanding of individual ministerial responsibility is to view the doctrine in terms of a number of 'elements'.

We might begin with the basic concepts of responsibility *for* something or other, and responsibility *to* someone or some body. With the first of these (responsibility *for*) we can say that people in government are responsible for the performance of certain functions associated with their particular roles ('role responsibility') and also for conducting themselves according to the laws of the land and the moral code of their peers ('personal responsibility').

Some overlap exists between these forms of responsibility. The personal responsibilities of a minister as a private citizen and as a Member of Parliament can, on occasion, seriously impinge on his or her effective functioning as a holder of specific role responsibilities in the department: in cases of ministerial implication in sex 'scandals' or financial corruption, for example. Thus Lord Lambton, the Under Secretary of State for Defence, and Lord Jellicoe, the Lord Privy Seal, resigned over a 'call girl' scandal in 1973; and Cecil Parkinson resigned as Secretary of State for Trade and Industry in 1983 following revelations about an affair between him and his former secretary, Sarah Keays. The same argument applies with reference to the position of a civil servant who must obey the law and abide by certain codified standards of conduct. George Pottinger, the Permanent Secretary to the Department of Agriculture and Fisheries in the Scottish Office, left the civil service in disgrace and was sentenced to five years' imprisonment on corruption charges in 1973 following an investigation into his financial relationship with the architect John Poulson.

While bearing in mind that the two forms of responsibility *for* are related, we would be justified in viewing the concept of personal responsibility, with its connotation of legally and morally appropriate standards of behaviour, as something which is reasonably distinct from the idea of role responsibility. The latter will be explored in more detail in the next part of this chapter. To sum up, responsibility *for* can be subdivided into two elements – *personal responsibility* and *role responsibility*.

Now, what about responsibility *to* ? Ministers and civil servants are responsible to other institutions and persons: in its most basic form, *to* Parliament in the case of the minister, and *to* a departmental superior, the minister and in certain circumstances Parliament in the case of the civil servant (see Chapter Four for a discussion of the concept of civil service accountability to Parliament). Let us use the term *accountability* when we mean responsibility *to* .

The notion of accountability itself implies the existence of a controlling agent, a person or body which, potentially at least, holds *sanctions* of blame or punishment over the office holder. In the case of the civil servant, the effective sanctions holders are their official superiors (although ministers may play a role in certain circumstances), and the main sanctions available are: reprimands, financial penalties, demotion or dismissal (see Chapter Five for more on the issue of sanctions).[1]

Having taken as our point of departure the fundamental concepts of responsibility to and responsibility for, we have now sketched out four elements of responsibility: personal responsibility, role responsibility, accountability, sanctions. If we view the doctrine of individual ministerial responsibility in this way, it is possible to state that a significant aspect of any minister's role responsibility and accountability will be related to the work of the departmental civil servants. He or she is accountable for certain actions taken by officials, and indeed for the failure of officials to act in some circumstances. The extent of this accountability is a moot point, which will be addressed in due course. Let us now consider the civil servant's role responsibility.

2. *The civil servant's roles*
The precise role responsibilities of specific civil servants are likely to vary according to the particular department in which they find themselves working. Nonetheless, it is possible to identify three

types of role which might be undertaken by officials.

First, civil servants are responsible, in general terms, for giving policy advice to ministers. Normally, such advice will come from the upper reaches of Whitehall's 'open structure', from officials ranked Under Secretary or above. Policy advice may come in a multitude of shapes and forms, but, broadly speaking, any senior civil servant will seek to keep his minister cognisant of possible legal, administrative and even political difficulties which might arise as a result of any given policy being followed. There is, of course, the crucial question about whether, in certain circumstances, the contribution of such policy advice may amount to something approaching the *creation* of policy. Does the nature of the civil servant's position allow him effectively to define the agenda within which the minister's policy decision must be made? This complex and controversial issue will be addressed in the final section of this chapter.

The second type of role undertaken by an official is that which involves the administration of departmental policy. Senior civil servants, usually in conjunction with ministers, will lay down guidelines for the implementation of policy. These will be conveyed, via Principals, to those charged with carrying out the detailed requirements of the policy at the point of contact with the public: the Executive and Clerical Officers.

The third type of role is that of departmental manager. Within this category we might include the creation of efficient organisational structures, personnel management, and the introduction of new systems and technology. While some ministers choose to become closely involved in this sphere, because they see departmental management as inextricable from the effective operation of the department as a policy machine, there is one aspect of management which is clearly the remit of the civil servant alone. This is financial accountancy, which is the particular responsibility of the Permanent Secretary. On entering office, every Permanent Secretary is issued with a Memorandum which sets out his duties as Accounting Officer for the Department.[2] The Accounting Officer must ensure that correct financial procedures have been followed, public funds have been properly safeguarded, ministers have been informed about the financial implications of policy proposals, and proper regard has been given to economy and the avoidance of waste.

This official is the department's principal witness who appears before the Publlic Accounts Committee to answer questions relating to the accounts. Responsibility for these matters is total. If a minister wishes to take a course of action which the Permanent Secretary considers to be financially irregular or improper, the latter must set out objections in writing. Should the minister decide to proceed nonetheless, the Permanent Secretary must comply with the ministerial command, but should inform the Treasury and the Comptroller and Auditor General. Only if this procedure has been followed will the Public Accounts Committee exempt the Permanent Secretary from responsibility for an item of departmental expenditure.

In 1975, a major clash developed between Tony Benn, Secretary of State for Industry, and his Permanent Secretary, Sir Antony Part, over the issue of the minister's policy of financial support for a number of workers' cooperatives. Part invoked the Accounting Officer's Memorandum. Benn strongly objected to the implication that he was authorising illicit expenditure, but he was particularly angered by the fact that a number of his senior officials seemed to use the difference of view about departmental spending priorities as an opportunity to brief his political opponents within the government and in the press, and mobilise opinion against their own minister. For Benn, this episode provided a key illustration of the innate conservatism of the civil service.[3]

3. Working relationships

A number of variables help to define the context of minister–civil servant working relationships. One of the most significant of these is the wide-ranging nature of the ministerial job. The role of a government minister may be viewed in terms of his or her position as policy leader, departmental manager, legislative pilot, and ambassador for the department in relation to Cabinet, pressure groups, and clients. Additionally, of course, most ministers also have responsibilities as Members of Parliament and party politicians. Given this range of roles and functions, the minister is likely to be under considerable stress.

A minister's tenure at the department is far from secure, in contrast to the permanent status of the officials. The minister may or may not possess a reasonable amount of 'clout' with political colleagues. The minister may be familiar with the details of the department's work before arriving, perhaps as a consequence of time spent as a Shadow Minister in that field, or personal experience acquired in the outside world. On the other hand, the new minister may be a comparative ignoramus in this respect. The minister could be a friendly character, possessing a natural ability to get on well with others, or might just be an aggressive, overbearing *prima donna* . All of these factors, and others (see the final part of this chapter) will have a bearing on the working relationship which is established between a minister and the departmental civil servants.

Some ministers operate in an atmosphere of almost continuous tension and conflict with their officials. For example, the behaviour of George Brown as a senior minister in the Labour Governments of 1964–70 became notorious. His Private Secretary at the Department of Economic Affairs offered to resign on seven separate occasions in the space of three months in 1964.[4] At a different level, the relationship between John Stanley (a junior minister at the Department of the Environment and the Ministry of Defence in the first two Thatcher Governments) and a range of officials across Whitehall was the subject of adverse comment during the controversy surrounding the Ponting affair in 1985.[5] (It should perhaps be noted that Stanley's ministerial career did not appear to be unfavourably affected by his reputation for dealing with his officials in an abrasive manner.)

By contrast, other ministers are able to establish cordial working relations with their civil servants. While this occasionally indicates that the minister has 'gone native' in the sense that he has been taken over by his civil servants, and by the departmental ethos, this need not always be the case. In some instances a collegiate relationship is etablished between the political and official elements at the top of a department. Senior Treasury officials, including the Permanent Secretary, Sir William Armstrong, enjoyed a close and constructive working relationship with Roy Jenkins, Chancellor of the Exchequer between 1967 and 1970. Armstrong has commented: 'We had a natural rapport. I don't remember anything where we were across each other.'[6]

Some ministers clearly take the view that their departmental officials are close allies in the constant in-fighting which takes place within the Whitehall 'village'. Thus, 'Rab' Butler who was, *inter alia* , Chancellor, Home Secretary, and Foreign Secretary during the Conservative Governments of 1951–64, was a man who got on very well with his civil servants.

> Even his scribbles on official minutes – 'No. 10 seems to be going mad' or 'Tell him to go to hell' – were modified neither by caution nor by inhibition; and sometimes his sense of fun would simply get the better of him, as when on a memorandum he approved of, instead of formally expressing thanks, he would simply draw a little Valentine – a heart with an arrow going through it pointing directly towards the initials of the writer.[7]

In a similar vein, Edward Boyle saw his officials at the Department of Education during the late 1950s and early 1960s as a valuable team of colleagues.

> I always found it desirable to try and fit in some time each week when I could talk to officials. . . . I always tried 'no holds barred' discussions with senior officials.[8]

For a minister like Anthony Crosland, who held senior posts in the Wilson and Callaghan governments in the 1960s and 1970s, the preferred working relationship with officials tended to be courteous yet detached. One of his Permanent Secretaries at the Department of the Environment, Sir Idwal Pugh, saw Crosland as a rather formal figure.

> He was always very relaxed with senior officials and showed us the most impeccable courtesy, but his reserve allowed no indication of what he was feeling. Early on I made up my mind simply to know him on paper. The ideal relationship between a Permanent Secretary and a Minister is when you meet late in the evening over a whisky or a cup of tea and talk about this and that. I never did with Mr Crosland. You can work with a minister either way. You become less committed if it is done more formally. It was all very *proper* . We would go into his room and sit on our side of the table. He'd say: 'This is the subject. These are the points.' We'd go through them. 'O.K.' We'd depart.[9]

Of course, the whole nature of a working relationship can change over time. Furthermore, the illustrations cited hitherto ignore the obvious point that a minister may have quite different working relationships with two or more groups of officials. This tendency on the part of ministers to distinguish between civil servants is apparent in the writings of the famous Labour ministerial diarists. Richard Crossman's battles with Dame Evelyn Sharp, his Permanent Secretary at the Ministry of Housing and Local Government, can be contrasted with the friendlier relations he enjoyed with some less senior officials.[10] Barbara Castle differentiated between two broad groups of officials in the Department of Health and Social Security:

> ...I was aware that the department is split into two different worlds: the conventional, change-nothing world of the top Establishment; the challenging, irreverent world of the press office and some of the younger officials.[11]

Her ambivalence towards the officials shines through her diary entry for 5 March 1975, which contains the comment:

> I get very fond of my civil servants (or at any rate some of them). The outside world has no idea how human they are.[12]

The most recently published diary by a former senior Labour minister is that of Tony Benn. While prepared to admit that a few of his younger officials were stimulating working partners, Benn became disenchanted at an early stage in his ministerial career with what he saw as the prevailing negative and unimaginative approach of most civil servants. The diary entries of Benn as Postmaster General chart his growing disappointment with the calibre of the middle-ranking departmental officials. On 7 December 1964,

> I had the first of my informal lunch meetings with thirteen people from the Building, Welfare and Transport departments. They sat round my table drinking beer and eating sandwiches and apples like a lot of middle-aged bankers on a church outing. There was not a spark of enthusiasm, imagination or excitement of any kind to be seen. I am really talent-spotting and even a person of average intelligence would shine out of that sort of group.[13]

On 25 January 1965,

> I had the internal telecommunications people to lunch today.
> I'm not sure these lunches are turning out to be much of a success.
> Occasionally one meets a bright chap, and Mr Jones who is head
> of the particular branch that I met, was undoubtedly one of the
> brighter characters but the rest seemed to me a bit scornful. The
> trouble with the Civil Service is that it wants a quiet life. The civil
> servants want to move slowly along the escalator towards their
> knighthood and retirement and they have no interest whatsoever
> in trying to develop new lines of activity.[14]

The examples cited here are necessarily limited and selective,
and it might be argued that there are as many types of
ministerial-civil service working relationships as there are variations
in the human character. However, on the evidence before us, we
could categorise the working relations between ministers and their
departmental officials in the following way:

Conflictual: ranging across a spectrum from the severe case of
Brown to the less marked yet still fundamentally abrasive relations
between Castle, Benn and their officials.

Detached: typified by the Crosland illustration.

Collegiate: as seen in the Butler, Boyle and Jenkins examples.

4. 'Policy is like the elephant'?

The whole question of the civil servant's role in the creation and
implementation of public policy is a thorny one. We have already
argued that the provision of policy advice to ministers and the
administration of policy form two of the civil servant's 'role
responsibilities'. However, the precise connection between the
departmental official and policy is difficult to identify.

In the course of interviews conducted with a number of ministers
and civil servants two broad views emerged from both ministerial
and official sources. One of these amounted to an admission that
civil servants do make a major contribution to policy decisions,
behind a department's closed doors. They 'fight for their corner' in
the discussions which take place, but once a decision has been
reached, whatever it may be, a sense of collective responsibility
descends on all concerned, and when the doors of the department
open, ministers and officials present a united front to the world in

defence of "the minister's policy". The other view held that the divide between matters of policy and administration is real, but strangely intangible. Hence the use of such phrases as: 'policy is what the next chap up is doing and administration is what the next chap down is doing' (a Permanent Secretary to the author) and 'policy matters are like the elephant – difficult to describe, but you know one when you come across it!' (variations on this theme were put to the author by several ministers and officials).[15]

The extent to which the balance of power between ministers and civil servants is tipped in favour of the officials is a matter of considerable debate. It is often argued that a competent and efficient minister who 'knows his own mind' and has clear policy objectives will have nothing to fear from departmental officials, who will be only too keen to implement his wishes. Should the minister have little or no clear idea about the main policies he or she wishes to pursue, then of course the bureaucratic machine will operate in such a fashion as to fill the vacuum with a sensible policy of its own. While there is likely to be a germ of truth in this argument, perhaps it is just a trifle simplistic in the sense that it overlooks the fact that senior civil servants are complex political actors in their own right, and will have opinions on policy which may conceivably differ from those of their minister. In these circumstances, the officials have several distinct advantages:

1 Ministers tend to be transient creatures. On average, they stay in posts for only two or three years. Civil servants, on the other hand, are likely to spend significant parts of their careers within particular departments or policy spheres.

2 Ministers have many roles to fulfil, and some of these will take them outside the department for considerable periods of time (up to two-thirds of the working week may be spent outside the department).[16] The officials who work with a minister are likely to be in the department almost all of the time.

3 Ministers may lack specialised expertise in relation to aspects of departmental activity, while the civil servants will have built up their specialised knowledge over the years, and may use this to control the flow of information to their minister.

4 Ministers may be temporarily (or permanently!) at odds with senior Cabinet colleagues, or the Prime Minister. As the experience of Tony Benn shows, departmental officials who

disagree with their own boss might seize on this political isolation in order to bring pressure to bear on the minister.

5 Ministers cannot implement their own policies. Policy implementation lies in the hands of civil servants who may delay or distort a policy initiative. In some cases, it might be enough for officials who oppose their own minister on particular issues to play for time until he or she moves on. Again, the Benn experience is opposite. Support for workers' cooperatives was scaled down by his successor at the Department of Industry in 1975, Eric Varley, and his questioning approach towards nuclear energy was rejected by the new Conservative Energy Secretary, David Howell, in 1979.

Taken together, these inherent advantages can be used to support what might be described as the 'dictatorship of the official' or 'conspiracy' theses. Again, in their purest forms, such views perhaps veer too far towards simplistic explanations for complex policy developments, but they should not be dismissed out of hand.

Those who criticise the civil service from left-wing and right-wing perspectives often pursue similar arguments, to the effect that since the Second World War officialdom has used its inherent advantages in order to assert itself in favour of centrist, consensus policies.

• From the left, the argument is that the civil service has acted as part of the political establishment or ruling class in order to maintain the *status quo* and neutralise the radical impulses of Labour governments as a whole, or of particular ministers such as Tony Benn. The social composition and outlook of senior officials is cited as evidence of the natural conservatism (or even Conservatism) of the civil service.[17]

• From the right, the argument is that the civil service became wedded to the economic and social strategies of the interventionist post-war governments, to the extent that it developed a 'closet Socialist' perspective, had a vested interest in 'big' government, and would act against any attempt to undermine its power and influence.[18]

Any student of the modern civil service must be familiar with the broad thrust of these arguments and interpretations. It is not necessary to subscribe in full to one or other of them, but a reasonably clear comprehension of the factors which underpin the power balance between ministers and civil servants is an important prerequisite for a better understanding of the Whitehall machine.

In order to develop our understanding of some of the main issues surrounding the ministerial–civil service relationship in the policy sphere, let us now look in turn at officials and departmental policy, at officials and central policy, and finally at the issue of politicisation of the civil service.

We have already seen that among the major criticisms which tend to be levelled against the civil service role in departmental policy are the assertions that officials are deficient in strategic awareness and political insight,[19] or that the civil service as a body is a malign influence with an unhealthy attachment to the *status quo*. Because of such criticisms, some senior government ministers (in most cases, only the Prime Minister) have in the past made use of special political advice to supplement or counter-balance the advice received from the civil service. However, in the 1960s a new trend emerged, which involved an attempt to move away from the old, informal system, and towards the formal establishment of the political adviser, as a temporary civil servant.

The use of such advisers by ministers in the Labour Governments between 1964 and 1970 remained limited, but the experience of those like Richard Crossman (who, as Secretary of State at the DHSS, brought Brian Abel-Smith from the London School of Economics to be his special political adviser) clearly reflected a changing approach to the question of the departmental 'irregulars'. In its evidence to the Fulton Committee in 1966, the Labour Party recommended a significant increase in the numbers of political appointments, and the development of a continental-style *cabinet* system for departmental ministers.[20] (Note that the concept of a *cabinet* of advisers for ministers should not be confused with the Cabinet which is chaired by the Prime Minister!)

Fulton accepted that there might be a case for the appointment of small numbers of political advisers to aid ministers, but rejected outright the concept of the *cabinet*. The introduction of such a system would undoubtedly have had a dramatic effect on the traditional relationship between ministers and their officials, particularly in the area of their respective role responsibilities for policy leadership and policy advice. There are various forms of the system. Even in the European countries where *cabinets* are common, no prescribed format exists: in some cases the *cabinet* contains only party political aides of the minister, while in others it consists solely of officials, hand-picked by the minister.

> In practice the *cabinet* is most likely to be composed of a mixture of people ... drawn from the department for their policy expertise and from the party for their understanding of its attitudes and priorities.[21]

The *cabinet* idea was also being considered in Conservative circles in the late 1960s. The year before his election victory, Edward Heath set up a 'Businessmen's Team' headed by Richard Meyjes from Shell, and including Derek Rayner from Marks and Spencer. In the aftermath of the 1970 election victory, this team suggested a full-scale review of the organisation of ministerial private offices, with a view to introducing a *cabinet* system. This proposal was resisted by the civil service, and the Prime Minister could not be convinced that it was desirable.[22]

Thus, by the end of the Heath Government, the trend towards using special political advisers had become further entrenched, although the idea of ministerial *cabinets* seemed to have been discarded.

The return of the Labour Government in 1974 brought a quite remarkable increase in the numbers of special advisers used by ministers. No fewer than 38 of them were appointed within months of the election victory, partly in response to the emerging view that senior mandarins had sabotaged much of the reforming zeal of the 1964–70 Governments. Harold Wilson issued guidelines which governed the appointment of advisers.[23] Although some senior ministers did not make use of the scheme, most departments had a couple of political advisers working closely with the Secretary of State.

The number of special advisers in Whitehall started to decline even before Wilson's retirement in 1976, partly because many of the initial appointments had been strictly short-term. However, after James Callaghan became Prime Minister the whole experiment came under fire. Like Wilson, the new occupant of 10 Downing Street valued his own team of advisers, but Callaghan was less than happy about the possibility of leaks springing from the ranks of the departmental advisers. Their conditions of service were tightened up, and their access to Cabinet documents restricted.[24] During this period the *cabinet* idea received another airing in certain circles (Tony Benn became increasingly attracted to the concept), but it remained on the drawing board while the more limited experiment with ministerial advisers waxed and waned.

Margaret Thatcher's arrival at Downing Street in 1979 brought a dramatic strengthening of the Prime Minister's personal system of advice (as will be illustrated in due course). As far as departmental ministers were concerned, however, it became more difficult to make use of special political advisers. Some ministers did take the opportunity to appoint advisers, usually bringing them over from the Conservative Research Department. However, it soon became clear that the Prime Minister was prepared to monitor very closely the number and type of advisers chosen by her ministers. Indeed, she apparently vetoed the choices made by some of her less favoured colleagues.[25]

The whole issue of policy support for ministers came under consideration again in 1985–86. A major investigation conducted by the House of Commons Treasury and Civil Service Select Committee found in favour of the idea of special political advisers, and came out in support of the *cabinet* concept. The Committee proposed that a *cabinet*-style body, to be called the 'Minister's Policy Unit' should be established on an experimental basis in a number of departments, in order to assess its effectiveness.[26] In the period following the publication of this report there were no indications that the Committee's proposals had been taken seriously.

Leaving aside the question of ministerial *cabinets*, what effect did the use of special political advisers actually have on the civil servant's responsibility for policy advice and implementation? In theory, the minister's role as policy leader in a department would be affected by the work of an adviser concerned to a significant extent with the formulation of policy advice. Correspondingly, the civil servant's role as policy adviser would be affected by the arrival of one or more 'outsiders'. In practice, however, the effect seems to have been negligible.

Notable exceptions can be mentioned. Roy Jenkins discovered that his role responsibility for policy leadership at the Home Office was supplemented to a considerable extent by the work of his special adviser, Anthony Lester. A barrister and a QC, Lester has been credited with the authorship of the laws on race relations and sex equality which Jenkins pioneered as Home Secretary.[27] Lester's impact on the role responsibility of Home Office officials for policy advice was understandably great, but the civil service resentment seems to have been minimised by his willingness to 'work with the grain' and avoid antagonising officials.

At the Departments of Industry and Energy (in turn) Tony Benn also found that his responsibility for policy leadership was supplemented by the use of special political advisers. Frances Morrell and Francis Cripps have, like Lester, been praised for making significant policy contributions. They wrote important White Papers in both departments, as well as providing the research which opened up the whole question of future nuclear energy policy. Unlike Lester, however, Morrell and Cripps found that their impact on the traditional civil service responsibility for policy advice was resented, to the extent that the internal affairs of the Department of Energy came to resemble 'trench warfare'.[28]

Aside from the rather isolated instances of genuine impact, epitomised by the cases of Lester, Morrell and Cripps, the effect of the new political advisers on civil service role responsibilities in the policy sphere was not as great as might have been expected. It seems clear that the explanation for this is to be found in the wider reasons for the failure of the modern 'experiment' with special advisers.

Opposition to a full-blooded *cabinet* system, wavering political commitment to the 'experiment', the desire of particular Prime Ministers to exert maximum control over their colleagues, civil service obstructionism, the lack of 'heavyweight' advisers – all of these factors combined to undermine the potential threat to the policy role of the departmental civil servant.

If the civil service has largely succeeded in maintaining its position as the major source of departmental policy advice in the late 1980s, the same claim can be made in the realm of central, strategic policy, albeit with some major qualifications and reservations. Here, the story has been one of erratic, but marked, political encroachments upon the civil service functions, but, ultimately, the maintenance of a key role for the senior civil service.

It is apparent, from even a cursory glance at the working of the Whitehall 'village', that the officials working in the Cabinet Office exercise considerable influence over the shape of strategic policy. This body is responsible for the planning of all business which goes before the full Cabinet and its Committees. Inevitably, such business must be planned weeks and even months in advance. The planning and manipulation of the Cabinet agenda is, therefore, to a large extent in the hands of the Cabinet Secretary (since 1988, Sir Robin Butler), although he will work closely with the Prime Minister in this and other respects.

There are 35 Cabinet Office civil servants working in the arena of strategic policy. Ministers wishing to raise major issues in full Cabinet or in one of the Committees must submit written outlines of their proposals to these officials. Through its Secretariat, which is divided into six sections dealing with Home Affairs, the Economy, Europe, Science and Technology, Security and Intelligence, and Overseas and Defence Policy, the Cabinet Office provides senior ministers with organisational support (agendas, minutes, circulation of documents) and also with policy briefs.

Add to this the image of Permanent Secretaries and senior officials across Whitehall holding regular meetings which effectively 'shadow' those involving their ministerial masters, as well as the pivotal strategic policy role performed by the odd 'super-mandarin' in the mould of Sir Robert Armstrong (Cabinet Secretary 1979–88, Joint Head of the Civil Service 1981–83, Head of the Civil Service 1983–88), and a picture emerges of the extensive civil service influence over strategic government policy.

While making allowances for all this, however, it is difficult to deny that Cabinet ministers, and especially the Prime Minister, have shown an increasing tendency to look beyond the civil service for central policy advice. Traditionally, of course, the challenges of war had provided opportunities for ministers to seek and utilise broad policy guidance from 'outsiders'. However, it was in circumstances of peace that an attempt was made effectively to circumvent the Whitehall networks, and allow strategic policy advice to be fed directly to Cabinet ministers via a Central Policy Review Staff (CPRS) manned by seconded civil servants *and* outsiders.[29]

This 'Think Tank', set up by Edward Heath in 1970, immediately aroused suspicion within the Whitehall departments. However, fears that the intellectual firebrands in the CPRS would be constantly second-guessing the advice emanating from the more conventional sources proved to be unfounded. Indeed, some rising stars of the civil service, such as Sir Robin Butler, were to discover that a spell in the 'Think Tank' did not damage their standing with either their political or their official superiors.

From a fairly early stage, it became clear that the CPRS could not achieve its stated aim of providing broad strategic policy guidance to the Cabinet as a whole. Instead, it settled into a 'routine punctuated by orgies', that is, the provision of occasional long-term policy papers in quite specific areas (such as the future of the British car industry 1975, the Diplomatic Service 1976, the welfare state 1982), combined with almost continuous advice on shorter-term issues. Instead of serving the Cabinet as a whole, the CPRS came to provide papers for the perusal of particular ministers (sometimes to their acute embarrassment, as with the review of the welfare state, which contained a broad range of options, some quite unthinkable, especially in an election year!)

The CPRS was always likely to depend on Prime Ministerial goodwill for its survival. While it fitted into Edward Heath's plans for a revamped Whitehall, it was often viewed by his Labour successors, Wilson and Callaghan, as a 'Heathite' device. Margaret Thatcher spent a term in Downing Street before deciding that the CPRS had failed to carve a clear role for itself, while exhibiting a dangerous tendency to leak. It did not come near to meeting her requirements as far as strategic overview of policy was concerned. The Thatcher instinct was for policy advice which fitted into her own ideological framework rather than that which stemmed from cold, objective analysis. The CPRS was abolished in the immediate aftermath of the Conservative election victory in 1983.

The demise of the CPRS did not result, as might have been expected, either in the creation of a formal 'Prime Minister's Department', or in an expansion of the Cabinet Office (although the latter did inherit some of the functions of the old 'Think Tank').

Instead, a trend which had already been apparent between 1979 and 1983 became more marked. Margaret Thatcher liked to have strategic policy advice centred on her, rather than on the Cabinet as a whole. During her first term in Downing Street she began to develop and orchestrate the components of the Prime Minister's Office and a few external 'Think Tanks', in order to suit her particular purposes. Her system of central policy advice was flexible enough for her to reject the need for a 'Prime Minister's Department'.

The Prime Minister's Office is really a collective term which was first afforded formal recognition in government publications in the mid-1970s. In fact, the Office has four components: the Private Office, the Political Office, the Policy Unit, and the Press and Information Office. The Private Office is staffed by civil servants (a Principal Private Secretary and six Private Secretaries), usually high-flyers on secondment from other parts of Whitehall. One of the Private Secretaries, Charles Powell, came to be credited with having a fair degree of influence in policy matters during the late 1980s. This Office is mainly concerned with providing the Prime Minister with a back-up facility for parliamentary activities (such as the preparation of speeches, statements, and answers to Questions), channelling memoranda from the departments of state to the PM (a role also performed by the Cabinet Office) and offering a personal secretarial service. A measure of the importance of the Private Office is the fact that the man who became Cabinet Secretary and Head of the Civil Service in 1988, Sir Robin Butler, previously served as Margaret Thatcher's Principal Private Secretary.

The Political Office was created by Harold Wilson in the wake of his 1964 election victory. Until 1979 this Office tended to be headed by publicly recognisable figures (Marcia Williams under Wilson, Douglas Hurd under Heath, Tom McNally under Callaghan), charged with the responsibility for keeping the PM in touch with party and broad political developments. Under Mrs Thatcher and John Major, the Political Office continued to be occupied by party rather than official figures, but they came to operate in the shadow of the people working in the Policy Unit.

The Policy Unit was another Wilson innovation, being formed on his return to Downing street in 1974. Bernard Donoughue was recruited from academia to become senior policy adviser and head of the Unit under both Wilson and Callaghan. The Unit is staffed by seconded civil servants and outsiders on 'attachment' to the civil service. It exists to provide the PM with medium-term to long-term policy analysis. Thatcher's Policy Unit developed slowly but steadily after 1979, consisting for a time of little more than the special adviser Sir John Hoskyns. As the Unit grew, Hoskyns became its head; when he left, he was replaced by Ferdinand Mount, in turn succeeded by John Redwood early in 1984. By the late 1980s, the unit was being headed by Brian Griffiths. He had six people working under him. In December 1990 John Major appointed the journalist, Sarah Hogg, as head of the Policy Unit.

What was more significant, and more worrying for the civil service than Thatcher's gradual elevation of the Policy Unit, was her use of special sources of advice in those policy areas which concerned her most. At the same time as she was closely monitoring the advisers appointed by her own ministers, she was cultivating her own strain of high-powered sages. The thoughts of these men were designed to supplement the strategic policy work being done by the Policy Unit, and to second-guess the advice coming to the PM from the departments of state. The first of the special policy advisers was Sir Alan Walters, an economist with distinct monetarist sympathies. His return to Downing Street, after a period of absence in the United States, led to a direct clash with the Chancellor of the Exchequer, Nigel Lawson, who resigned in 1989 on the specific issue of Walters's impact on the government's economic policy.

Special advisers had been appointed in other areas of policy such as defence and foreign affairs. Additionally, Margaret Thatcher had established at an early stage a small Efficiency Unit headed by her special adviser on civil service efficiency, Sir Derek (later Lord) Rayner, then from 1983 by Sir Robin Ibbs, and from 1988 by Sir Angus Fraser.

The final component of the Prime Minister's Office had its origins in the 1930s. The Press and Information Office, which provides the Prime Minister with public relations advice and is the medium through which 'off the record' briefings are given to Lobby correspondents, had traditionally been headed by two types of

Press Secretary. Clement Attlee and Harold Wilson selected sympathetic journalists for the job (Francis Williams and Joe Haines) while other Premiers, including Edward Heath and James Callaghan, opted for civil servants who were specialist Information Officers.

The Downing Street Press and Information Office was transformed into a particularly assertive arm of the Prime Minister under the active leadership of the erstwhile civil servant, Bernard Ingham. Combining the talents of journalist and civil service Information Officer, he did not hesitate to pit his office's resources against attempts by both parliamentary and media elements to damage the image of the Prime Minister and Government. His committed style in the course of crises such as the Westland affair obliged Margaret Thatcher to argue in his defence that Ingham's role was compatible with his status as a civil servant. Ingham was an early victim of John Major's Premiership; his replacement, Gus O'Donnell, was an Information Officer from the Treasury.

In addition to these, the components of the Prime Minister's Office, mention must be made of the external 'Think Tanks'. Margaret Thatcher's preference for policy advice which was of an avowedly ideological nature meant that her appetite was unlikely to be completely satisfied by the rather dispassionate type of analysis emanating from the CPRS and the departments of state. Thus the elevation of the political components of the Prime Minister's Office. For the same reason, she came to make use of her free access to three external 'Think Tanks', all of which are exponents of New Right philosophy: the Centre for Policy Studies (set up by Thatcher and Keith Joseph in the 1970s), the Institute of Economic Affairs, and the Adam Smith Institute.

Mrs Thatcher's habit of drawing extensively on the political elements of the Prime Minister's Office and the external 'Think Tanks' for strategic policy advice does not imply that the upper reaches of the civil service now have a limited role in this respect. However, it seems reasonable to conclude that in the 1980s the balance moved perceptibly in the direction of political rather than official sources of central policy guidance. This was epitomised by disclosures about the roles performed by various groups and individuals in the period leading up to the publication of the

January 1989 White Paper on the future of the National Health Service. In addition to the submissions made by the relevant departments, Brian Griffiths and the Downing Street Policy Unit, the Centre for Policy Studies, and the Adam Smith Institute all produced papers. While it would be wrong to suggest that their ideas were accepted in full, their impact could be seen in the White Paper's proposals for 'internal market' mechanisms to be established in the NHS.[30]

A major requirement of a 'permanent', career civil service is that it should be able to provide advice and support to governments of all political persuasions. Consequently, the civil service must be seen to be politically neutral. During the 1980s, as never before, serious questions were regularly posed regarding both the existence and the desirability of this neutrality. After leaving the Downing Street Policy Unit, Sir John Hoskyns launched a strong attack on the Whitehall ethos.[31] He argued for an influx of political appointees in the upper reaches of the civil service. In the Hoskyns model, the top layers of the departmental structure would be lopped off to facilitate the appointment of temporary 'civil servants'.

How can you have a radical government without radically minded officials? Difficult problems are only solved ... by people who desperately want to solve them.[32]

Hoskyns' critique was attacked by an array of retired or retiring Permanent Secretaries, as well as a number of government ministers.[33] The prospect of the British civil service being laid open to an American-style 'spoils system' found little favour. The flexible nature of the present system, and the loss of expertise which would result from an abandonment of the traditional departmental structures, were cited as sound reasons for leaving things as they were.

The speed of events ensured that the Hoskyns debate soon seemed redundant in any case. It was Margaret Thatcher's good fortune to be in Downing Street at precisely the time when a substantial proportion of the post-war generation of mandarins reached the age of retirement. Between 1979 and 1985, 43 Permanent Secretaries and 138 Deputy Secretaries retired.[34] Due to the knock-on effect of these departures, a vast number of senior appointments had to be made. While it would not necessarily be true to state that party political motivations were at work when the new men were promoted, it is clear that the Prime Minister's personal approval played a much bigger part in the selection process than had been the norm.

The conventional routine was that the nominees of the Senior Appointments Selection Committee were passed to Downing Street for final approval, which had been a formality under previous Prime Ministers. However, in the period when significant numbers of appointments were being made, the SASC was chaired by Sir Robert Armstrong, the Cabinet Secretary, who had been issued with precise guidelines regarding the type of mandarin the Prime Minister would find acceptable. Unlike most premiers, Mrs Thatcher made it her business to know the people at the top levels of the civil service and she was, in consequence, well placed to oversee the promotion of those who met with her approval. The Whitehall grapevine had it that the vital quesion being asked about potential appointees was 'Is he one of us?' This was taken to imply a commitment to the 'can-do' ethos of Thatcherism rather than any obvious affiliation to the Conservative Party.

Nonetheless, some of the appointments aroused controversy. For example, the promotions of Michael Quinlan, Clive Whitmore and Peter Middleton as, respectively, Permanent Secretary to the Department of Employment, the Ministry of Defence, and the Treasury, were said to bear the Prime Minister's imprint to a particularly marked degree. The high profile cut by Bernard Ingham and Sir Robert Armstrong in politically sensitive affairs such as Ponting, Westland and 'Spycatcher' served to add fuel to the fires of the politicisation debate.

Statements emanating from the Opposition indicated that many of the senior officials who had served the Thatcher Government would have the status of 'damaged goods' in the event of the change of administration. One senior member of the Shadow Cabinet stated that a new Labour Government would

> look closely at what's been happening in Whitehall under Margaret Thatcher. . . . We've seen Mrs Thatcher pursue the 'one of us' syndrome right across the whole administration in this country including the Civil Service. And I think there must be a number of people in Whitehall now in senior positions who are, frankly, compromised by that – and they'd have to go.[35]

The perceived politicisation of the upper reaches of the civil service since 1979 would be overcome, according to this critic, not by the introduction of the political appointees favoured (for different reasons) by Hoskyns, but by a more open system of appointment. This idea has also found favour with a variety of individuals and groups, including Peter Hennessy, a keen and perceptive observer of the Whitehall 'village',[36] the House of Commons Treasury and Civil Service select committee,[37] and the Royal Institute of Public Administration.[38]

The administration trainee intake ('fast stream' for university graduates) would be reduced gradually while the top three grades would be staffed increasingly by means of open advertisements. Appointments would be made not by ministers, but by the Civil Service Commission. While this prescription for change is unlikely to be supported by those who oppose any tampering with the traditional Whitehall appointments and promotion system, it has the merit of acknowledging the realities of modern government without opening the door to an unrestrained 'spoils system'.

4 Civil Servants and Parliament

The relationship between civil servants and Parliament is governed by the constitutional doctrine of individual ministerial responsibility. It was noted in Chapter 3 that this doctrine establishes the framework for the minister–civil servant relationship, and the relationship between the government machine and Parliament. Accountability was seen to be a key element of the doctrine. A strict interpretation of individual ministerial responsibility places definite limits on the accountability of departmental civil servants. They are accountable for their role responsibilities to their own superiors within the official hierarchy, and to their ministers. However, with the singular exception of the department's Accounting Officer (normally a Permanent Secretary), the doctrine, in its purest form, offers no recognition to the concept of direct civil service accountability to Parliament. Instead, officials are indirectly accountable, through the medium of their ministers, who answer MPs' questions regarding the activities of the 'faceless', 'anonymous' civil servants.

There must be some doubt whether this strict interpretation of doctrine ever fully corresponded with reality. The 'facelessness' and 'anonymity' of the civil service was never complete: certainly, the work of senior mandarins such as Trevelyan, Fisher, Hankey, Bridges and Brook was widely recognised in Westminster. However, the partial nature of official accountability was undeniable. It was only in the mid-1960s that a serious challenge began to develop to the concept of a limited, indirect civil service accountability to Parliament. Before examining the impact and implications of this 'new regime' of parliamentary scrutiny, let us outline the 'old regime', the traditional methods of parliamentary scrutiny of the executive machine.

1. Traditional methods of parliamentary scrutiny

As the machinery of government expanded, an array of formal and informal devices developed, with the purpose of allowing parliamentarians to bring government ministers to account for their policies and the actions taken by their departments. These devices included private communications between MPs and ministers, Questions, various types of parliamentary debate, standing committees set up to examine Bills clause by clause, and a few important select committees (such as the Public Accounts Committee, the Estimates Committee and the Select Committee on the Nationalised Industries). Each can be said to have implied a degree of civil service accountability to Parliament, albeit through the media of ministers. For example, an MP who writes to a minister about a constituent's problem will have his letter handled by an Assistant Secretary, who will draft a reply subject to ministerial approval.

Parliamentary Questions are undoubtedly the most famous of the traditional methods of scrutiny. Questions come in a number of different forms, including notified oral Questions (with un-notified supplementaries) put to ministers on the floor of the Commons in a rota system, Questions for written answer, and urgent Private Notice Questions. All of these have an impact on the work of government departments. The task of overseeing the process of preparing answers to Questions normally falls to a Principal working either in the private office of the Secretary of State or, more usually, in a special parliamentary section of the department. When compiling the information needed for an answer, the Principal will consult a number of colleagues working in various parts of the department. The 'PQ' work will take priority over all other business. The draft answer, along with supporting information, is passed up the departmental hierarchy. Normally, the minister concerned, along with his Private Secretary and the Permanent Secretary, will consider the draft and notes which, in the case of a 'starred' Question (for oral answer), will provide information on points which might arise in supplementaries. When answering in the Commons, the minister will be watched by his Private Secretary, sitting in the official box at the side of the Chamber, who will make a note of any last minute adjustments made by the minister, as well as the supplementaries.

Thus, the Question is designed to bring about the accountability of ministers for their role responsibilities. However, officials also find themselves under scrutiny, even if not from Parliament directly. Each Question attracts ministerial attention to the work being done by the departmental officials. The minister brings an internal form of accountability to bear on the civil servants. The latter are effectively answering to their minister for the conduct of their own role responsibilities as policy advisers, departmental managers and departmental administrators: the minister, in turn, answers to Parliament. One Permanent Secretary, in a department which attracts a large share of Questions, summarised this concept of civil service accountability to Parliament via ministers.

> The primary function of departmental civil servants is to support the Secretary of State in meeting his responsibilities. The accountability of officials themselves, in support of their ministers, is total. At its lowest level, this total accountability is reflected in the processing of around 30,000 MPs' letters per annum in this department, and about 5,000 Parliamentary Questions.[1]

Parliamentary debates, like Questions, come in different forms, but can be broadly divided into general and legislative debates. They may have a number of purposes, but will usually serve to bring a minister to the despatch box to explain, defend and account for departmental policies and activities. As with Questions, the real target in a debate might be the minister's officials. While viewing debates as a vicarious form of scrutiny, and by no means an adequate substitute for face to face contact, some MPs do believe that civil servants can be reached through the medium of parliamentary debate. This point can be supported with reference to the comments of three former ministers, who spoke about their aims as backbench MPs when contributing to general and legislative debates:

> It's no good talking to the minister on the front bench. He ignores it, even if he understands it. What one is trying to do is put the fear of God into the civil servants.

> One despairs of influencing ministers. . . . When I speak, I speak to the civil servants who have so much of the power.

The senior civil servants, they're the chaps I'm after. The thing is getting senior civil servants to come to the minister three days after the debate saying 'Minister, we ought to point out to you: Mr _____ had a point in that speech he made.[2]

Another form of legislative scrutiny occurs in standing committees. Most government Bills are sent 'upstairs' between second reading and report stage, to be considered by these committees. Here, the partial and indirect nature of civil service accountability to Parliament is at its most obvious. Standing committees carry out the task of scrutinising Bills (which have been drafted in large measure by officials) by discussing each clause and suggesting possible amendments. However, witnesses are not called, and there is no cross-examination of either ministers or civil servants. An MP eager to question a knowledgeable official, who may be sitting only a few feet away while a standing committee is in session, has to ask and receive an answer to the question through the minister. Truly a case of 'so near, yet so far'.

Traditionally, select committees have offered an additional form of parliamentary scrutiny of the executive. The oldest select committee, the Public Accounts Committee, was established in 1861. Chaired by a senior opposition MP with ministerial experience in the Treasury, the PAC examines senior figures from Whitehall on matters arising from the departmental accounts, which have been audited by the Comptroller and Auditor General and his staff in the National Audit Office. The uniqueness of this organ of scrutiny is that it can not only question ministers and senior civil servants, but it is the sole medium through which officials can be held directly accountable to Parliament in a legal and constitutional sense. The Accounting Officer of a government department (in almost every case, the Permanent Secretary) is the principal witness who appears on behalf of the department (see Chapter 3 for a summary of the procedure to be followed by an Accounting Officer who wishes to be exempted from responsibility for a particular item of departmental expenditure). Permanent Secretaries clearly feel the weight of this responsibility. One has described the 'sharply interrogative' atmosphere which prevails at meetings of the PAC.[3] Another placed the scrutiny exerted by the Comptroller and Auditor General at the top of a list of concerns which lingered at the back of his mind as he went about his daily work.[4] Every Permanent Secretary prepares in great detail for appearances before the PAC.

> The Permanent Secretary ... will spend about three weeks concentrating solely on PAC work ... such a concentrated dose of information relating to particular aspects of his Department's work can do no harm to any Permanent Secretary. Indeed, most of them believe that as a result they are better informed ....
> Occasionally such preparatory work takes the Permanent Secretary to sites of projects he would not otherwise visit, to meet members of his department he would not otherwise have met.[5]

It is important to stress the unique nature of the PAC within the array of traditional select committees. Other committees, however prestigious (and a certain amount of prestige did come to be attached to the work of bodies such as the Estimates Committee 1912–70, and the Select Committee on Nationalised Industries 1956–79) could call for witnesses and documents, but had no power to enforce the direct accountability of civil servants. Officials could be questioned by committees, but, ultimately, they appeared as ministerial mouthpieces, and could certainly not be questioned about any matter deemed to be in the realm of 'policy'.

2. A new regime of parliamentary scrutiny

The traditional methods of parliamentary scrutiny were imperfect in many respects. As the machinery of government became more sophisticated and complex, especially after the Second World War, the task of exercising an adequate degree of scrutiny and control became more difficult. The Crichel Down affair in 1954 highlighted the weaknesses in the system for securing redress of citizens' grievances against the might of the bureaucracy. If Parliament was to fulfil its role as an effective 'watchdog', it was going to have to cultivate a louder bark and sharper teeth. Ministers would have to be held to account for their responsibilities more regularly and in greater depth. Perhaps MPs would have to devise some means of bringing civil servants into a more direct relationship of accountability to Parliament?

During the second term of Harold Wilson's first Labour

government, a new phase of Britain's constitutional history began. The Parliamentary Commissioner for Administration, in operation by 1967, together with a range of new experimental Commons select committees (starting in 1966) represented a potentially significant supplement to the existing forms of parliamentary scrutiny. In addition to the traditional methods of scrutiny, there were new devices designed to enhance the accountability of the government machine to Parliament. A new regime of Parliamentary scrutiny emerged after 1966.

Some of the impetus for reform had been generated outside the confines of Whitehall and Westminster. The British lecture tour of the Danish Ombudsman, Professor Hurwitz, in 1958, brought some publicity for the campaign which had been launched the previous year by Justice, the British section of the International Commission of Jurists. In 1961, a committee of Justice, chaired by Sir John Whyatt, published a report which put forward a set of proposals for a British ombudsman.[6] Although the Whyatt report was relatively cautious, the Conservative government of Harold Macmillan dismissed its proposals on the grounds that

it would not be possible to reconcile them with the principle of Ministerial responsibility to Parliament ... there is already adequate provision under our constitutional and Parliamentary practice for the redress of any genuine complaint of mal-administration, in particular by means of the citizen's right of access to Members of Parliament.[7]

However, the Labour Party, in opposition, became committed to the introduction of a British ombudsman, and the first Parliamentary Commissioner for Administration was appointed in 1967. Great stress was placed on the fact that Britain had a *Parliamentary* Commissioner, rather than an ombudsman on the original Scandinavian model. Thus, there was to be no direct access to the PCA by members of the public with grievances against government departments. Instead, complaints about 'maladministration' would be filtered through a Member of Parliament. The intention was to avoid overloading the system with a deluge of complaints, and to facilitate the creation of a specialist 'Rolls Royce' service. From the outset, therefore, the Commissioner's role was to be a servant of the House of Commons. Backbench MPs were to have at their disposal a new organ of scrutiny, which would supplement their existing weaponry. As the Leader of the Commons, Richard Crossman, put it when commending the PCA idea to the House:

> for the first time a complaint to a backbench Member of Parliament about maladministration in any Department may precipitate a searching and detailed investigation, including the close examination of everyone concerned, from the top to the bottom of the Department and the examination of all the relevant secret Departmental files. This is considerable change. What happened previously in a few rare cases now becomes a continuous possibility ....[8]

The PCA and his team were to be equipped with powers to secure the accountability of ministers and their officials to Parliament. Under the terms of the 1967 Act, the Parliamentary commissioner could require any minister or departmental official to produce all documents relating to the particular case under investigation and, if necessary, to answer questions informally or under oath. Ministers or officials could not be required to produce documents or answer questions relating to the proceedings of the Cabinet or its committees, but the PCA could demand access to any other papers. In November 1967 a Select Committee on the PCA was set up to review the operation of the new device, and to exert pressure on departments which might be reluctant to implement the Commissioner's findings in any given case.

Since 1967 the PCA has acted as a significant agent of accountability, and has had a particular impact on the accountability of civil servants in the Whitehall departments and their outposts.[9] A relatively straightforward procedure is set in motion by the PCA when presented, via a Member of Parliament, with a citizen's complaint against a department. First, the substance of the complaint is examined in order to ensure that it conforms with the Commissioner's understanding of 'maladministration' (the precise definition of this term has been the subject of a long-running debate) and to check that the complainant has no form of legal or quasi-legal redress (that is, via a court or a tribunal) open to him or her.

Having satisfied himself on these grounds, the PCA then

approaches the department concerned, armed with formidable powers to search out material and summon witnesses. The investigation is conducted without the glare of publicity. The department's Permanent Secretary is given notification of the complaint which has been made. At that stage, two things happen. The departmental official with responsibility for PCA affairs, the 'nominated officer', liaises between the Commissioner and the department, guiding the PCA staff to the relevant files and the civil servants most closely connected with the case. In the meantime, while the PCA and his staff go about the business of investigation, the department conducts its own internal investigation, designed to provide the Commissioner with the official response to the complaint.

It is this internal investigation, as much as anything, which establishes the point that the advent of the PCA brought with it a substantive increase in the accountability of civil servants. Whereas a Parliamentary Question or an MP's letter to the minister would attract the attention of senior officials only if important policy issues were concerned, every PCA case is ultimately handled by the Permanent Secretary. Senior civil servants have testified that this duty is taken very seriously:

> When he [the PCA] does conduct an investigation in the department, I write back to him. I don't sign blandly at the end of the letter. I only sign the reply after I have really looked at the case – so his investigation does mean something.[10]

> His work is given serious consideration by the department. When a case reaches my desk, I read every document in the file. If one considers the possibility of some thirty Permanent Secretaries doing this across Whitehall, the impact of the ombudsman must be seen as considerable. The highest ranking civil servant in a department will look at the case with a dispassionate eye and offer his carefully considered judgement.[11]

The PCA's staff continue their investigations by consulting the relevant case papers and conducting interviews with the civil servants involved. Occasionally, there is a need for ministers to be interviewed, usually by the Commissioner himself.

In general, successive Parliamentary Commissioners have viewed the quasi-judicial aspect of their authority (the power to administer oaths and *compel* the attendance of witnesses/ production of documents) as a last resort. Commissioners maintain a relatively informal style of investigation. However, this does not detract from the importance which departmental officials attach to the work of the PCA. A number of civil servants have made use of their statutory right, under provisions of the 1967 Act, to request legal or other (normally trade union) representation in the course of a PCA investigation.

The process of investigation complete, the Parliamentary Commissioner will have reached one of three conclusions. He may have found no evidence to support the claim that the department concerned had been guilty of maladministration. He may have identified no maladministration as such, but invite the department to re-examine its rules and procedures, and perhaps to look with some sympathy at the position of the complainant. Finally, of course, he may have discovered clear evidence of maladministration on the part of the department. In this case, if he is also convinced that real injustice has been inflicted on the complainant, the Commissioner will seek to ensure that the department takes acceptable remedial steps. Ultimately, in cases where a department fails to redress the complainant's grievance to the satisfaction of the Commissioner, he can expect his political arm, the Select Committee on the PCA, to take up the cudgels on his behalf.

The final stage of the investigation involves the compilation and publication of the PCA's report. A draft of this will first be shown to the Permanent Secretary of the department involved, in order to allow for the identification of any basic factual errors. Thereafter, the final version of the report is sent to the MP who referred the complaint, and to the Permanent Secretary. An anonymised version of the case is then included in the PCA's quarterly report to Parliament. Figures 4.1 and 4.2 give some indication of the scale and the outcomes of PCA investigations during 1989.

The impact of the PCA on civil service accountability is to be seen most obviously in the departments which regularly attract the highest numbers of complaints: the Departments of Social Security, Employment, Environment, the Home Office and the Inland Revenue (see Figure 4.3). The work of the PCA improved the accountability of civil servants to their superiors in the official hierarchy and to their ministerial masters. However, the real

Figure 4.1: PCA casework 1989

Cases received	677	Reports issued	126
Cases carried forward from 1988	260	Cases discontinued	11
		Cases rejected	502
		Cases carried forward to 1990	298
TOTALS	937		937

Source: Parliamentary Commissioner for Administration, Annual Report, 1989, HC 353 1989–90, para 76.

Figure 4.2: Outcomes of PCA investigations 1989

Complaints upheld	48%
Complaints justified but not upheld*	42%
Complaints not justified	10%

* In these cases, the PCA criticised at least some aspects of the department's handling of matters.

Source: Parliamentary Commissioner for Administration, Annual Report, 1989, HC 353 1989–90, para 73.

Figure 4.3: Main departments investigated by the PCA 1989

Departments which had 20 or more complaints directed against them:

Department	Complaints	Investigations
Social Security	223	88
Inland Revenue	90	16
Environment	45	1
Home Office	34	14
Transport	28	4
Employment	26	6
Customs and Excise	21	4

Source: Parliamentary Commissioner for Administration, Annual Report 1989, HC 353 1989–90, para 74.

innovation was the enhancement of civil service accountability to Parliament.

The work of officials in the middle and lower ranks of any department could attract the attention of their superiors in a way which would scarcely have been conceivable before the introduction of the PCA. The serious treatment which departments accorded to investigations served to emphasise the point that the work of the Parliamentary Commissioner had introduced an additional check on officials. In this way, the internal accountability of civil servants was improved. This point can be extended. Ministers would also learn more about the work being done by civil servants at various levels in their departments, as a result of the PCA's work. This could only have the effect of enhancing ministerial accountability.

However, with the arrival of the PCA, the direct accountability of civil servants to the third, external, agency came a step nearer. The PCA introduced a limited, but definite, movement in the direction of civil service accountability to Parliament. Limited, in the sense that the Commissioner and his staff were not parliamentarians as such, but servants of Parliament. Nonetheless, when officials answered questions before the PCA, they answered to Parliament. These were not simply senior civil servants answering the questions of the Public Accounts Committee in their very special capacity as departmental Accounting Officers. These were officials from every rank and standing answering questions relating to their role responsibilities for policy advice, departmental management, and the administration of policy. Furthermore, in certain circumstances, there would be the possibility that civil servants might be called to account for their actions before the real parliamentarians sitting on the body which represented the Commissioner's political arm, the Select Committee on the PCA. This could be significant:

> in cases where (as the department sees it) there are arguments, but not absolutely conclusive arguments, for refusing the remedy sought by the Commissioner, the knowledge that a decision not to do as he wishes will certainly mean the appearance of the Permanent Secretary, fully briefed, before the Select Committee, is a consideration that must sometimes help to tip the balance in favour of the complainant.[12]

Figure 4.4: New House of Commons select committees

1. 1966–70
1966–67: Agriculture
        Science and Technology
1967–68: Agriculture
        Science and Technology
        Education and Science
1968–69: Agriculture
        Science and Technology
        Education and Science
        Scottish Affairs
        Overseas Aid and Development
        Race Relations
1969–70: Science and Technology
        Education and Science
        Scottish Affairs
        Overseas Aid and Development
        Race Relations

2. 1970–79
Expenditure Committee (Sub-Committees: Defence and External Affairs, Environment, Trade and Industry, Education, the Arts and the Home Office, Social Services and Employment, General Sub-Committee).
Science and Technology
Overseas Development
Race Relations and Immigration
Education and Science (until 1971)
Scottish Affairs (until 1972)

3. 1979–
Agriculture
Defence
Education, Science and Arts
Employment
Energy
Environment
Foreign Affairs
Home Affairs
Industry and Trade
Scottish Affairs*
Social Services†
Transport
Treasury and Civil Service
Welsh Affairs

* Not reappointed after the 1987 Election, due to a dispute about composition.

† Split into distinct Health and Social Services Committees at the end of 1990.

After 1967 officials at every level might find that their actions formed the subject of a report sent by the PCA to a Member of Parliament who had passed on a constituent's complaint and, subsequently, in the Commissioner's reports to Parliament collectively. This represented a clear enhancement of civil service accountability to Parliament.

Similarly, it can be argued that the development of Commons select committees over the period since 1966 has also marked a subtle change in the relationship between civil servants and Parliament. This period witnessed three distinct chronological phases in the evolution of the new select committees. Between 1966 and 1970 there was an experiment with 'specialist' subject and departmental committees. The years 1970 to 1979 saw the surviving committees from the first phase working alongside a new Expenditure Committee. A major reform in 1979, introduced by the new Conservative Government's Leader of the House of Commons, Norman St John Stevas, brought into being a rationalised 'system' of fourteen departmentally based select committees. Figure 4.4 presents a complete list of the select committees which operated within these three phases.

A glance at Figure 4.4 should be enough to confirm that the post-1979 select committees offered a broad range of scrutiny over government activities. Fourteen was the highest number of committees which had operated concurrently since the inception of the new regime. Furthermore, after 1979 the committees were more clearly based on departments of state (monitoring anything from a single department to a group of departments) than their predecessors, some of which had been explicitly department-based, while others were subject-related.

The remit of the fourteen committees was deliberately vague: 'to examine the expenditure, administration and policy of the principal government departments ... and associated public bodies'.[13] This seemed to be an implicit invitation to the committees to define their own roles and objectives. However, some objections were voiced in 1979, and afterwards, regarding the government's failure to go beyond the traditional formulation of the powers of select committees to send for persons, papers and records. None-theless, in the most general terms, the expanded jurisdiction of the committees after 1979 meant that the accountability of the executive machine to the House of Commons had been enhanced. More committees covering more ground produced a quantitative increase in accountability. The quality of scrutiny provided by the committees could be affected by a number of variables, including the calibre of committee chairmen; attendance and turnover of members; partisanship; size, nature and relative political importance of the department being monitored; and access given to personnel and documents. Bearing these qualifications in mind, it is possible to state that the work of the select committees improved the accountability of civil servants for the full range of their role responsibilities, to their official and ministerial superiors, and, most importantly, to Parliament.

Within departments, the prospect and fact of select committee investigations served as a catalyst for enhanced internal accountability. The committees imposed a significant workload on departmental officials. Early in the life of the new committee system, an exercise conducted by the Civil Service Department showed that, in the course of the year beginning February 1980, an estimated 12,039 man-days had been spent by officials on the preparation of written memoranda and the provision of briefings related to committee inquiries.[14] This figure excluded the time needed for officials' appearances before the committees.

Work of this nature was done by civil servants at every level of the departmental hierarchies, involving a supervisory checking mechanism which served to heighten the internal accountability of officials to their civil service superiors and to their ministerial masters. The major innovation brought about by the select committees was, however, the development of *de facto* civil service accountability to Parliament. As the numbers of witnesses being called before the committees increased, especially after 1979, it became clear that giving evidence 'was the business of officials about $6\frac{1}{2}$ times as intensively as it was the business of ministers'.[15] A study conducted by the Management and Personnel Office revealed that the civil servants most in demand were those in the middle and upper ranks.[16]

Of course, none of this necessarily proves that civil service accountability to Parliament was improved as a result of the work done by the select committees. Reduced 'facelessness' does not equal increased accountability. Indeed, a cautionary note should be sounded before this argument is taken further. Early in the life of the post-1979 select committees an assertion of the prevailing influence of traditional views about the place of the civil servant came in the form of a 'Memorandum of Guidance for Officials' appearing before committees.[17] This document, which was compiled by Edward Osmotherly of the Civil Service Department, was actually a revised version of existing guidelines, but its appearance at an early stage in the life of the new committees seemed to serve as a reminder of the facts of Whitehall life.

The Osmotherly Memorandum precluded civil servants from giving evidence about matters which lay outside the jurisdiction of the committees, such as the workings of Cabinet committees and the legal departments. More than this, however, the Memorandum made it clear that while the committees would, of course, be tolerated and even accorded some respect, they would not be allowed to upset the traditional way of doing things. Thus, while officials were advised to be as helpful as possible to the select committees, certain qualifications were made to this general rule. Cost had to be taken into account when compiling information for the committees. The twin constitutional doctrines of collective and individual ministerial responsibility were to be beyond challenge. Information about inter-departmental exchanges on policy issues was not to be disclosed lest it shed light on the manner in which a minister had consulted his colleagues. More importantly, in several closely linked passages the Memorandum offered guidance which, if fully adhered to, could have effectively short-circuited the operation of the committees as genuine organs of scrutiny. Officials were not to give evidence on or discuss 'the advice given to ministers by their departments' or 'questions in the field of political controversy'.[18] This seemed to be an attempt to preserve the traditional anonymity of the civil servant, by distancing him or her from the consideration of matters of policy (despite the fact that policy advice formed a major part of civil service role responsibility), while simultaneously acquiescing in the requirement for civil servants to appear before select committees. It was also an attempt to preserve constitutional fiction.

As the role of government in many areas of society and economy increased, and departments became larger, so the gap narrowed between matters which could clearly be termed 'policy' and those which could clearly be termed 'administration'. Two things followed from these developments. The first was that the Commons had to add to the existing mechanisms for bringing ministers to account. The second was that civil servants would have to become increasingly accountable directly to Parliament through the organs of the new regime, as well as indirectly through their ministers.

In this light, the Osmotherly Memorandum took one step forward by recognising that advice which influences policy decisions is given to ministers by civil servants. However, it took two steps back by maintaining that this advice should not be subject to scrutiny by the select committees.

> Officials should be ready to explain what the existing policies are and the objectives and justification as the Government sees them, for those policies, and to explain how administrative factors may have affected both the choice of policy measures and their implementation. It is open to officials to make comments which are not politically contentious but they should, as far as possible, avoid being drawn ... into discussion of alternative policy. If official witnesses are pressed by the Committee to go beyond these limits, they should suggest that the questioning be addressed, or referred, to Ministers.[19]

This encouragement to civil servants to stall before committees was given in the clear knowledge of the existence of a grey area between 'policy' and 'administration', What is the difference between advice, based on 'administrative factors' which leads to a choice of policy options, and straightforward policy advice? Ostensibly there would seem to be some difference, but on closer examination it is obvious that the effect of each type of advice is the same, and is unavoidable: to define the agenda for decision-taking.

The net effect of the Osmotherly Memorandum was to leave the question of the accountability of civil servants hedged with uncertainty. Clearly, they were accountable (*de facto*) on a more regular basis, directly to Parliament as well as indirectly via their ministers. The question of what they were to be accountable for remained clouded by the fact of the increasingly hazy divide between policy and administration, coupled with the intimation by

Osmotherly that the civil servant's role responsibility as a policy adviser would remain out of bounds for the select committees.

Osmotherly was never revoked, but the operation of the post-1979 select committees, and a series of highly publicised cases involving individual civil servants, served to expose the inherent contradictions of the Memorandum. The *de facto* accountability of civil servants to Parliament seemed to be consolidated, even in the face of Osmotherly's *de jure* statement of non-accountability in the realm of policy advice. Nonetheless, this process of consolidation was problematic. Examples abound of civil servants hiding behind the skirts of Osmotherly and 'ministerial responsibility'. Hugo Young and Anne Sloman spoke to a large number of officials for the BBC Radio series, 'No, Minister', and found some officials prepared to go

> into some remarkable intellectual contortions to make it clear that before a select committee it's not really they who are being examined – but someone who isn't even in the room.[20]

Such an approach was positively encouraged by the terms of the Osmotherly Memorandum, and by some Permanent Secretaries, such as the one who told the author that

> When answering questions before a Committee officials must be careful to avoid giving their personal opinion. It would be true to say that officials are given considerable scope to give their advice to the minister behind the closed doors of the department, but once they leave the department a kind of collective responsibility applies, with officials defending the agreed policy whatever their personal views have been.[21]

Not surprisingly, this sort of attitude was viewed as sheer obstructionism by some select committee members. As one senior committee-man commented:

> They [civil servants] will always duck behind a minister when it suits them, but if they duck too sharply they will be questioned further.[22]

Sir Kenneth Couzens, former Permanent Secretary at the Department of Energy, held strong views about committee members who chose to push civil servants to answer questions.

His comments say much about the attitude of at least some members of the Whitehall hierarchy towards Parliament in general and the select committees in particular:

> The select committees should avoid the tendency to become arrogant in their dealings with departments. They should be allowed to inform themselves, but not to play God. The pomposity of it sometimes passes all belief. They are not my employers! When they start browbeating civil servants, I regard that as intolerable.[23]

Perhaps not surprisingly, all of this leads some MPs to despair of civil servants as witnesses. However, fortunately not all officials cling to the protective skirts of Osmotherly as tightly as the more insecure denizens of the Whitehall departments. A senior Treasury official, Peter Kemp, who has made numerous appearances before the Treasury and Civil Service committee, was quite positive about his experiences.

> Contrary to a popular view, civil servants often actually rather enjoy appearing in front of a select committee. I do myself. We want to try to be helpful to the committee ... we do have views and it would be quite wrong had we not. The committees must be interested in these views.[24]

Correspondingly, most MPs who are actively involved in the work of the committees would testify to their value as bodies which enhance civil service accountability. Renee Short, who chaired one of the most diligent and influential committees in the early 1980s, the select committee on Social Services, believed that the effect of the committees had been to keep officials 'on their toes'. She felt this could be done, not only through the initial questioning during a committee inquiry, but also by bringing civil servants back at the end of the investigation to face questions about the problems which the committee had identified within departmental systems and policies. While agreeing that civil servants could, on occasions, be 'cagey', Mrs Short believed this could usually be overcome.[25]

This positive view of the impact of the select committees on civil service accountability is shared by no less a figure than the former Permanent Secretary at the Treasury and joint Head of the Civil

Service, Sir Douglas Wass. He has referred to the 'inexorable logic' of the growing responsibilities of ministers and the concomitant desire on the part of Parliament to concern itself

> directly with the point in the Minister's department where detailed responsibility lies. To the extent that this happens and a bypass comes to be built around the minister which creates a direct route between the serving official and Parliament, certain consequences seem to follow .... Although my generation of civil servants has been brought up to regard every act taken by an official as an act in the name of the Minister, our successors may therefore have to be prepared to defend in public and possibly without the shield of ministerial protection, the acts they take.[26]

Just before he retired, he could discern genuine signs of this taking place.

> There have been several developments in recent years in this direction .... We now have standing machinery in the form of the Departmental Select Committees which are able to examine official witnesses in public on matters of public and parliamentary interest.[27]

For Sir Douglas, the new select committees seemed to signal the need for a decisive move away from precisely the type of minimalist interpretation of civil service accountability contained in the Osmotherly Memorandum. And if such a view could be found at the top of that bastion of official conservatism, the Treasury, it seems fair to assume that it had reached into other bureaucratic corners. Each time a committee pressed a recalcitrant official into talking sensibly about his or her work, instead of retreating behind a constitutional smokescreen, a certain amount of Osmotherly's credibility was destroyed.

That credibility suffered an extremely serious battering in the wake of a series of events in the mid-1980s. The question of civil service accountability emerged as a major political issue at the time of the Ponting affair. The prosecution and acquittal of Clive Ponting, an Assistant Secretary in the Ministry of Defence, in January 1985, after he had leaked official documents, became something of a *cause célèbre* for those who argued that the civil servant should be in a positive relationship of accountability to Parliament as well as to his or her departmental superiors and ministers (Ponting had sent to Tam Dalyell MP documents relating to ministerial handling of the controversy surrounding the sinking of the *General Belgrano* during the Falklands War).[28]

Even before the Ponting case, the prosecution, early in 1984, of the Foreign Office clerk, Sarah Tisdall, had indicated the seriousness which the government attached to civil service leaks. Tisdall's rationale for leaking, and her chosen method, placed her in a weaker position than that of Ponting, but the principle was the same in each case. Furthermore, it could be argued that Tisdall was rather unfortunate to find herself in the dock at the Old Bailey, given the fact that another civil service 'mole' with similar motives managed to escape this fate. Ian Willmore, an administration trainee in the Department of Employment, left the civil service on his own terms, without being prosecuted, because, beyond his own statement which was made only after he had been offered immunity from prosecution, the government lacked any clear proof that he had been the culprit.[29]

Together, these cases helped to open up the debate about the accountability of civil servants. The wider ethical implications of this debate will be discussed in the next chapter, but our concern here is with the immediate issue of parliamentary accountability. In the aftermath of Tisdall, Willmore and Ponting, the First Division Association and other civil service unions came out in favour of an official code of ethics and an appeals procedure to rationalise the relationship between ministers, civil servants and Parliament. Sir Douglas Wass suggested a compromise between the existing, closed system of civil service accountability, and the establishment of clear and accepted lines of accountability to Parliament. He favoured independent appeals procedures, perhaps based on a civil service 'Ombudsman' or an 'Inspector General'.[30]

The government continued to place great faith in the traditional procedures. Robert Armstrong, Cabinet Secretary and Head of the Civil Service, responded to the developing problem in two ways. In August 1983 he sent a letter to all Whitehall Permanent Secretaries, demanding that they exercise greater vigilance in order to stem a spate of leaks. Ironically, this letter was itself leaked, and it appeared in *The Guardian*. Following the Tisdall, Willmore and Ponting cases, Armstrong was obliged to offer a more constructive statement which might help those officials who faced a dilemma when confronted with possibly illegal, unconstitutional or even simply politically controversial aspects of their work. However, his Note of Guidance on the Duties and Responsibilities of Civil Servants in Relation to Ministers (the 'Armstrong Memorandum'), was a blunt restatement of constitutional orthodoxy.[31] Its basic theme was that civil servants are accountable only to their own superiors in the administrative hierarchy, and to ministers.

House of Commons select committees were to come into sharp conflict with the doctrine set out in the Osmotherly and Armstrong Memoranda during the Westland affair. Again, the ethical implications of this case will be examined in the next chapter, but it must be noted here that Westland raised the issue of the role and function of select committees in relation to departmental civil servants. The government refused to allow the officials involved in the affair to be questioned by the Defence committee, and the latter chose not to push the issue, being prepared to accept an appearance by the Cabinet Secretary in lieu of the officials. There followed a critical report from the Defence committee[32] and an inquiry by the Treasury and Civil Service committee into the implications of this affair for ministers and civil servants. In its report, the Treasury and Civil Service committee attacked the decision to shield officials involved in the Westland affair from legitimate investigation by a select committee.

> The officials concerned might well have welcomed an opportunity to explain their actions in public (which would not we stress have been in conflict with the confidential nature of advice to ministers). It would also have enabled Parliament to consider who was responsible for any mistakes and who ought to have been held accountable.[33]

The government's response took the form of an attempt to roll back some of the most important advances which select committees had made in the period since the mid-1960s. The Osmotherly rules were apparently to be tightened up to the point where civil servants would be quite useless as witnesses. This was immediately recognised as a regressive step, designed to eliminate the possibility of senior departmental officials being closely questioned about their own conduct, and that of ministers. In the face of considerable protests in Parliament, John Biffen, the Leader of the House, was obliged to alter course, and give an assurance that civil servants would continue to be questioned in detail by select committees.[34] As a result of these developments, Robert Armstrong issued a revised version of his Memorandum.[35] However, in its fundamentals, this merely reiterated the arguments of the initial document.

There remains a significant gap between the constitutional orthodoxies peddled in times of crisis by the senior figures in the executive and administrative machine, and the real world of the select committees where direct civil service accountability to Parliament is being nurtured on a day to day basis. Having touched upon certain aspects of the Tisdall, Willmore and Ponting affairs, it would now be appropriate to expand on the major ethical issues which these, and other cases, raise.

5 Ethics in the Civil Service

This chapter examines ethics in the civil service, with reference to three main themes. First, using a broad definition of ethics, the conditions of service of civil servants will be outlined. Second, some comments will be made about the circumstances in which officials can be identified and punished through the use of sanctions in cases where there has been a breakdown in personal or role responsibilities. Finally, as a development upon the comments made about accountability in earlier chapters, the relationship between the work of civil servants and the 'public interest' will be examined.

1. Conditions of service

While charting the historical development of the civil service, it was pointed out that key factors in the general conditions of service for officials were 'neutrality' and 'permanency'. Thus, in discharging their role responsibilities civil servants are required to

> serve the duly elected Government of the day, of whatever political complexion. It is of the first importance that civil servants conduct themselves in such a way as to deserve and retain the confidence of Ministers, and to be able to establish the same relationship with those whom they may be required to serve in some future Administration.[1]

The words are those of Robert Armstrong, who was Head of the Civil Service between 1981 and 1988.

These central characteristics of the British civil service, 'neutrality' and 'permanency' (or, in Armstrong's terms, 'non-political' and 'disciplined career service'), raise a number of important issues. An alternative to 'permanency' would be the adoption of a 'spoils system' of some description, whereby incoming ministers would be able to appoint senior officials on a political basis. Some of the implications of this will be discussed in the next chapter. Of greater concern to us in this chapter is the ethical issue of 'neutrality'. At a later stage, we shall address the specific question of the rights and responsibilities of the civil servant who believes that being a loyal, 'neutral' official might, in certain circumstances, conflict with deeper matters of principle.

Beyond these very general conditions of service, there are more detailed conditions which relate mainly to the civil servant's personal responsibility and conduct, and are set out in a variety of official documents. Chief among these are the Prevention of Corruption Acts 1906 and 1916, the Public Bodies Corrupt Practices Act 1889, the Civil Service Pay and Conditions of Service (CSPCS) Code, and the Establishment Officer's Guide (which applies to the more senior ranks of the service).

The CSPCS Code superseded the old Estacode, which was first formulated in 1928. The Code sets out standards of conduct and specifies the disciplinary sanctions which apply when these standards are infringed. Among the issues addressed by the Code are: procedures for the reporting of bankruptcy, insolvency, arrests or convictions; caution on the acceptance of gifts, rewards, awards and prizes; restrictions on political and business activities. In addition, individual departments may lay down specific rules for their own officials.

The general intention which underpins these principles of conduct is that of expanding the personal responsibilities which each civil servant has as a private citizen, to the point where there can be (if the rules are adhered to) no misuse of his or her privileged position by any official. Hence, as far as business activities are concerned, there is no objection to civil servants holding private investments provided any shareholding does not raise the issue of conflict of interest with an official's department. No official may hold a directorship in a company which has a contract with his or her department, except in extraordinary circumstances (for example, if the official sits on the board of the company as the government's nominee). Civil servants are free to purchase surplus articles of government property, provided they do not obtain unfair commercial advantage over members of the public who may also be interested in purchasing the articles.

One of the most controversial aspects of civil servants' conditions of service relates to post-retirement appointments. During the 1970s and 1980s substantial numbers of senior civil servants retired or resigned from posts in Whitehall, only to take up very well-paid jobs in business and commerce. For example, when he retired in 1979, the former Cabinet Secretary, Lord Hunt, took up directorships with Prudential Assurance, Unilever, and the Banque Nationale de Paris. The Head of the Home Civil Service until 1981, Lord Bancroft, took up non-executive directorships with Bass, Rugby Portland Cement, Grindlays Bank and Sun Life Assurance. On his retirement from the Permanent Secretaryship at the Ministry of Defence in 1983, Sir Frank Cooper became a director of a number of companies, including United Scientific Holdings, a prominent defence contractor. Further examples, running into thousands of cases, were to be found through the civil service hierarchy.[2]

In dealing with this issue, governments attempted to strike a balance between preserving the rights of civil servants to pursue second careers, and safeguarding the public interest. In particular, there seemed to be an obvious need to ensure that officials did not bestow unfair advantages on prospective employers, either while still in office, or by providing detailed information about their former departments' affairs once in their new jobs.

In 1975, the long-standing rules governing the acceptance of outside appointments were revised. Permanent Secretaries were to be obliged to ensure that there was a gap of three months between resignation or retirement and taking up a business job. An Advisory Committee on Business Appointments (composed of people from outside the civil service) was to advise the Prime Minister on post-retirement appointments involving the top three civil service grades. In other cases, departmental ministers would have powers of discretion. In 1980 the CSPCS Code was amended to include a rule to the effect that officials ranked Under Secretary and above are required to obtain government permission before accepting business jobs within two years of resignation or retirement.

In practice, only a tiny proportion of the thousands of applications made under these rules are ever rejected. Even where permission is refused, this has no legal effect.[3] In 1984 the Treasury and Civil

Service Select Committee recommended a substantial tightening-up of the rules.[4] It proposed:

- a ban on senior officials having discussions with prospective employers during the last year of service before retirement;
- a ban on senior officials taking up private sector posts within five years of retirement or resignation;
- a more powerful role for the Advisory Committee;
- limitations on those matters for which former officials could assume public responsibility in their new jobs;
- withdrawal of pensions in cases where rules were flouted.

The government's response, in March 1985,[5] completely rejected the Committee's proposals, on the grounds that there was no evidence of abuse of the existing rules, and that the introduction of more rules would serve only to restrict freedom of movement between the public and private sectors.

Conditions of service, in generalised and detailed form, have become matters of particular concern for civil service trade unions. These bodies, which operate in a federation within the Council of Civil Service Unions (CCSU), reflect the diverse nature of the service itself. Thus, the First Division Association, representing the higher echelons of the Whitehall departments, sits under the same CCSU umbrella as the Civil Service Union, which represents cleaners, messengers, security officers and telephonists. Members of the Institution of Professional Civil Servants are mainly scientific and professional staff, while members of the Civil and Public Services Association are on clerical and secretarial grades.

Negotiations between the various trade unions (operating through the medium of the CCSU) and the employers (leading Permanent Secretaries and other senior officials), take place within the framework of the Whitley Council system of joint consultation. The Whitley Report, published during the First World War, had envisaged an extended system of joint consultative councils, giving representation to both management and trade unions, as a remedy for bitterness and unrest in Britain's industrial relations. In the event, 'Whitleyism' took root only in the sphere of the public service, as industrial managers and trade unions ignored the recommendations regarding joint consultation. Government, presenting itself as a model employer, oversaw the establishment of Whitley Councils across the public sector.

Consultations on pay, conditions of service, and related matters take place within the National Whitley Council (NWC), which deals with issues affecting all departments, and Departmental Whitley Councils (DWC), dealing with issues affecting individual departments.[6] In practice, the NWC now meets rarely, DWCs meet annually, and most serious business is conducted within sub-committees of the main bodies.

The atmosphere in the Whitley Councils gradually became more confrontational in the late 1960s as the new leaders of civil service unions began to question the conventions which underpinned 'Whitleyism'. It has been argued that,

> Once civil service unions start behaving like other unions – affiliating to the TUC, threatening industrial action, criticizing the government's policy towards public sector pay (and how can civil servants fight for more pay in an era of cash limits without doing precisely that?), talking about setting up political funds– then Whitleyism is dead, in spirit if not in body.[7]

The first civil service strike took place in 1973, and a nine-week pay dispute in 1979 resulted in a substantial victory for the unions. Increased action by the trade unions in the early 1980s was to produce a particularly controversial backlash from the Thatcher government. A major pay dispute broke out in 1981. In the course of this, the trade unions called on their members at the Government Communications Headquarters (GCHQ) in Cheltenham to join their colleagues in taking strike action. As a result, GCHQ, which provides signals intelligence as part of the government's security system, was temporarily closed down. In the aftermath of the dispute, the government at first attempted to reach an agreement with the unions to prevent further action of this kind. However, quite unexpectedly, in December 1983, the government announced that trade union membership was to be banned for GCHQ staff (financial compensation was offered for the loss of individuals' legal rights). The announcement of the ban, which surprised some senior government ministers as well as the trade unions, set off a protracted legal dispute in which the government ultimately triumphed, albeit at the cost of further embittering industrial relations in the civil service as a whole.

2. Naming and blaming: the use of sanctions against officials

Earlier, it was argued that civil servants have personal and role responsibilities, for which they are constitutionally accountable to their official superiors and ministers. The sanctions which might be imposed on an official in any given case of a breakdown in responsibility are: a formal reprimand, financial penalties, demotion or downgrading, and dismissal from the service.

In attempting to analyse the use of sanctions against officials, the observer encounters a number of obstacles. The annual collection of civil service statistics provides information about the numbers of officials who retired or died, but masks the precise number of dismissals within the category 'other leavers'. Attempts to persuade individual Whitehall departments to divulge data on these matters almost invariably meet with the response that 'such information is not readily available and could only be obtained by diverting our limited staff resources from other duties.' Careful study of the limited information which does emerge from Whitehall, however, allows us to compose a general picture of the usage of sanctions in the civil service.

In the majority of cases in which sanctions are used against officials, the catalyst is a failure in personal responsibility. By far the most senior civil servant to have been subject to sanctions in the modern period was George Pottinger, the Permanent Secretary to the Department of Agriculture and Fisheries in the Scottish Office. Along with a number of other figures in public life, he had become intimately involved in the affairs of the corrupt architect, John Poulson. Pottinger

> drove a Poulson car, wore Poulson suits, went on Poulson holidays, travelled on Poulson, ate on Poulson, stayed at hotels on Poulson, visited the theatre on Poulson, received his Christmas cheer from Poulson, and eventually lived in a Poulson house.[8]

Pleading ignorance of Estacode's rules on conflict of interest, Pottinger was sentenced to five years' imprisonment (reduced by a year on appeal) on corruption charges in November 1973, and he left the civil service in disgrace. Alfred ('Jack') Merritt suffered a similar fate after servicing Poulson's needs while working as the Ministry of Health's Principal Regional Officer. He was fined

£2,000, given a twelve-month suspended sentence, and dismissed from the service in 1974.

At lower levels of the service too, there are clear instances of sanctions being imposed for failures in personal responsibility. When a junior official from the Department of the Environment's Property Services Agency was tried at the Old Bailey in March 1982 on charges of bribery, he alleged that such abuses were rife, and had been going on for a period of years. An inquiry was mounted, and the next year it was revealed that 61 PSA officials had been dismissed because of their parts in fraudulent and corrupt activities which cost £100,000 in the period 1976–82.[9]

The CSPCS Code has as its overriding concern the personal rather than role responsibilities of officials. Although the sanctions permitted under the Code are intended to apply in cases of failure in relation to both types of responsibility, the Code itself represents an outline of the personal responsibilities of the civil servant. Of course, failures do take place in the sphere of role responsibility, but there is (or can be?) no written code which defines such responsibilities in detail: the interpretation of 'failure' in this sphere can be problematic. Even when clear cases of failure do occur, when mistakes have obviously been made, it is all but impossible to discover which sanctions have been imposed on the official wrongdoers by the effective sanctions-holders, their departmental superiors. The organ of parliamentary scrutiny which is most concerned with civil service role responsibility, the Parliamentary Commissioner for Administration,

> is not empowered to prosecute, or order the prosecution of delinquent officials, or begin disciplinary proceedings against them or even publicly to reprimand and officially warn them about their conduct . . . when the Commissioner criticises departments or individual officials in cases where faulty administration was not identified or acknowledged before his intervention, if the matter is serious enough, no doubt disciplinary action follows that would not have been taken but for his investigation. Parliament and the public, however, know nothing of this.[10]

Moreover, it might be added that ministers will almost certainly leave the disciplinary proceedings in the hands of their senior departmental officials.

To an even greater degree than in the sphere of personal responsibility, civil service role responsibility is a grey area as far as sanctions are concerned. We are left to make what we can of the few cases in which, after obvious failures had taken place, it seemed reasonable to raise the question of sanctions. One of the most striking cases centred on the operation of the Crown Agents between 1967 and 1974. A host of senior civil servants in two departments of state, at the Bank of England and in the Exchequer and Audit Department, in addition to the Agents' officials themselves, were engulfed by this financial catastrophe. However, there is no record of any sanctions having been imposed on the officials who were faulted by the report of the Croom-Johnson Tribunal which investigated the affair.[11] In part, this can be explained by the fact that some of the senior civil servants whose failings caused and then exacerbated the plight of the Crown Agents (which required the injection of some £225 million of public funds to save it from insolvency in the mid-1970s) were no longer in office by the time the Tribunal's report was filed in 1982. Most notably, this included Sir Claude Hayes, the Senior Agent, and Alan Challis, the Director of Finance. In addition, neither of the two ministers openly criticised (Dame Judith Hart and Lord Holderness) were still in office by the time of the report's publication, and it might have been argued that punishment of civil servants in these circumstances would have been unjust. Furthermore, a number of people were criticised for relatively minor errors, and this did not prevent a few of them going on to occupy highly prestigious posts in Whitehall.

Nonetheless, even allowing for these factors, it does seem remarkable that no sanctions of any description should have been imposed after a financial disaster which precipitated criticism of three Permanent Secretaries and two Under Secretaries at the Ministry of Overseas Development, a Second Permanent Secretary and two Deputy Secretaries at the Treasury, a Deputy Governor and a Chief Cashier at the Bank of England, a Chief Auditor and a Deputy Director of Audit at the Exchequer and Audit Departmant, and eleven senior officials at the Crown Agents. Only one official was suspected of having been lax in the sphere of his personal as well as his role responsibilities, and he had died in 1977. It was perhaps indicative of the relative importance attached to personal as opposed to role responsibilities that *The Times* could issue a perceptible sigh of relief on the morning following publication of the Croom-Johnson report: 'Incompetence Not Corruption'.[12]

An even more controversial case, and one which went to the heart of the question about the proper distribution of blame between ministers and their officials, was the Vehicle and General affair. This vast insurance company's finances had been a matter of concern in the City for a number of years, but its collapse in 1971 and the consequent substantial losses suffered by one million policy holders, seemed to take the government totally by surprise. The James Tribunal, which inquired into the circumstances surrounding the collapse of a company towards which the government had statutory responsibilities, named and blamed three officials in the Department of Trade and Industry's Insurance and Company's division for their failure to forestall the collapse.

Christopher Jardine, an Under Secretary, was found to have been negligent and incompetent,[13] while two Assistant Secretaries, CJ. Homewood and D. Steel, were severely criticised.[14] It seemed inevitable that the question of sanctions would arise. However, the two Assistant Secretaries retained their positions in the DTI and, while it is true that Mr Jardine was effectively demoted, the sanction was introduced in such a convoluted fashion that it hardly appeared to be a sanction at all (he 'retired' and was later re-employed in a more junior capacity in another part of the public service.)

One clue to the reasoning behind the use (and non-use) of sanctions in this case came from a former senior official in the DTI. He said that the way in which the James Tribunal focussed on the three officials

> distressed us all . . . where I feel the Tribunal was slack was in its failure to question the responsibility and role of the Deputy Secretary.[15]

Perhaps in this instance the guilt complex of the senior civil servants was a factor in the limited application of sanctions. Perhaps too, the fact that ministers escaped unscathed from the official report, played a part.

The James Tribunal's implicit conclusion was that no blame for the government's failure to forestall the Vehicle and General collapse could be attributed to any minister. This seemed to belittle the broad role responsibility of ministers for maintaining effective lines of communication within their departments, in order to enable them to be kept aware of gathering storms such as the developing crisis at this large company. Furthermore, the fact that the Secretary of State for Trade and Industry, John Davies – who was a man with a significant accumulation of business experience to his credit – failed to pick up from the City grapevine that which his departmental officials were unable to tell him, passed without comment in the Tribunal's report.

In the wake of Vehicle and General, the whole debate about the relative culpability of ministers and civil servants was opened up. In 1954, following the Crichel Down affair, the then Home Secretary, Sir David Maxwell Fyfe, attempted to draw a distinction between those actions taken by civil servants in accordance with explicit instructions from, or broad guidelines laid down by, ministers, and those actions which ministers either could not have been expected to know about or which were taken without ministerial approval.[16] In the former case, ministers would be expected to 'protect and defend' the official or officials concerned: there would be no naming and blaming of civil servants. In the latter case, it would be sufficient for ministers to give an account of what had happened to Parliament. Although Maxwell Fyfe did not specifically refer to ministerial resignations, his remarks were widely interpreted as laying upon ministers the duty of 'protecting and defending', up to and including the point of resignation, officials who might find themselves in the situations described.

Maxwell Fyfe's informal guidelines seemed to break down in the Vehicle and General case. Ministers found that they were obliged only to give an account of what had occurred, but were not to be seen as having been culpable, on the grounds that officials had failed to keep them informed. Thus, John Davies, the Secretary of State:

I think it is one of the sadder aspects of this whole matter that his (Under Secretary Christopher Jardine's) perhaps over-scrupulous application of the system of delegation led him to deprive himself of the protection that a reference upwards would have afforded him.[17]

In fact, as has already been pointed out, Davies in particular might reasonably have been expected to know something about Vehicle and General without placing undue reliance upon the work of his department's Insurance and Companies Division. This episode saw ministers successfully escape a share of culpability on the rather shaky grounds that, in Maxwell Fyfe's terms, the pending demise of a company with one million policy holders, towards which the government had statutory responsibilities, was not something they could have been expected to know about. Ministers could, and did, turn to the report of the James Tribunal in support of this defence. James placed an extremely narrow construction on his remit, and consequently failed to pay much attention to the role of ministers as opposed to that of officials. Ministerial files stretching back as far as 1961 were consulted, but no ministers were actually questioned by the Tribunal.[18]

During the Commons debate on Vehicle and General, the Home Secretary, Reginald Maudling, put forward his own interpretation of how culpability should be apportioned between ministers and officials.

> A minister cannot say in this House 'I am sorry. We made a mess of it. It was not my fault. Mr So-and-So, the Assistant Secretary got it wrong that day.' One cannot do that . . . . Ministers are responsible not only for their personal decisions but also for seeing that there is a system in their departments by which they are informed of important matters which arise.[19]

This echoed the speech of that other Home Secretary, Sir David Maxwell Fyfe. If Maudling's words were to be applied to the specific case of Vehicle and General, his ministerial colleagues at the DTI should have borne a share of the blame. However, Maudling then veered spectacularly from the straight and narrow path along which he had been striding so purposefully. He claimed that ministers could not be expected to supervise every aspect of their departments' work, and he attempted to draw a parallel between the million and a half personal letters he received annually as Home Secretary, and the work of the DTI's Insurance and Companies Division. By the end of his speech, Maudling seemed to be seeking the best of both worlds: conceding that ministers might theoretically be culpable in the Vehicle and General case, but maintaining that they should not be blamed, since the James Report had exonerated them.

Maxwell Fyfe's guidelines could not be said to have survived the trauma of Vehicle and General intact. That major case created a significant element of doubt about whether informal rules concerning the apportioning of blame between ministers and civil servants could operate in practice. Pious ministerial statements in the Maxwell Fyfe mould seem to have a very limited value once political careers are at risk. The fallibility of such informal guidelines was further exposed in the wake of the escape by nineteen Republican prisoners from the Maze Prison in September 1983.

When the report of the official inquiry into the incident (the Hennessy Report) was published a few months later,[20] the prison Governor was specifically blamed for this major failure in security, and the head of the Security and Operations Division of the Prison Department in the Northern Ireland Office was also criticised. The Governor later resigned. Civil servants and ministers at higher levels of the structure were not criticised. In spite of this, the Secretary of State, James Prior, and his Parliamentary Under Secretary, Nicholas Scott, came in for severe press and parliamentary criticism. Prior based his defence on the claim that no policy decisions had contributed to the failings at the Maze. This placed a rather limited construction on the role responsibility of ministers in the Northern Ireland Office, and did not really address the question of the role responsibility of the civil servants. The comment of *The Times* was scathing:

> A malaise as pervasive as this is shown to have been, in an executive branch of the public service so close to the security of the state, is a matter of ministerial responsibility, not as direct, but just as real as for any policy decision. The policy/adminis-tration distinction provides no refuge in a debacle as large as that. It does not dispose of the question of a ministerial resignation.[21]

There were to be no ministerial resignations or indeed sanctions against civil servants above the level of the prison Governor. Prior and Scott retained the support of the Prime Minister (a key factor in any case where the issue of ministerial resignations arises) and, with a few exceptions, that of their backbenchers. Armed with copies of the Hennessy Report, the ministers and their senior civil servants were able to ride out the storm.

The cases we have examined so far illustrate the point that civil servants can be placed in a form of double jeopardy. In some instances, they seem to be 'faceless', 'anonymous' officials, who are able to escape blame when things go wrong, by passing the buck. At other times, they seem liable to be treated unfairly, to be left to carry the can for ministerial or other failings. Further evidence of this was provided by the Westland affair (which we shall be touching upon in a slightly different context in the next section of this chapter).

At the height of this episode, in January 1986, a group of civil servants working in Number 10 Downing Street and at the Department of Trade and Industry were involved in a politically inspired conspiracy to leak information designed to discredit Michael Heseltine, the Defence Secretary. In the event, it was to be Colette Bowe, the Director of Information at the DTI, who actually carried out the leak (albeit with some moral qualms). Carefully selected extracts from a letter written by the Solicitor-General, Sir Patrick Mayhew, were released to the press, without his approval. This action was designed to cast doubt on the legality of a statement which had been made by Heseltine, who was lobbying for a 'European' solution to the problems of the Westland helicopter company against the wishes of Prime Minister Thatcher and Leon Brittan, the Trade and Industry Secretary.

The leak was carried out by Bowe, on behalf of her Secretary of State, Brittan, and with the connivance of Number 10 Downing Street. The civil servants at the DTI (Bowe; John Mitchell, the Head of Air Division; and John Mogg, Brittan's Private Secretary) had been told by the Chief Press Secretary at Number 10 and the Prime Minister's Private Secretary (Bernard Ingham and Charles Powell respectively) that disclosure of the letter was necessary, but could not be done through Downing Street. Both the Prime Minister and Leon Brittan were clearly implicated, directly or indirectly, in this underhand affair. Brittan later admitted that he 'would not suggest for a single moment that my instructions were anything other than followed'.[22] This comment, made in the aftermath of the affair, can be interpreted as an attempt by a former minister (he had resigned by this stage) to shield his departmental officials from criticism by asserting that they were doing his bidding. Nonetheless, it was inevitable that the Commons Select Committee on Defence, when investigating the Westland affair, would examine the activities of all the major actors in the drama, including the civil servants.

However, the government blocked the committee's attempt to question the officials who had been involved in the leak. In spite of this, having examined the evidence available, the committee named and blamed the officials at the DTI and Number 10 Downing Street. The committee's report was scathing:

> Whatever authority the five officials involved may have thought they had . . . they were wrong to disclose it or to connive at its disclosure. Yet we understand from [Cabinet Secretary and Head of the Civil Service] Sir Robert Armstrong's evidence that no disciplinary action is to be taken against any of the officials concerned. We find this extraordinary.[23]

Ironically, one of the civil servants criticised in the report, John Mogg, was promoted to the rank of Under Secretary only weeks later!

In the belief that some civil servants had been treated shabbily by their ministerial and official superiors over the years, the civil service trade unions (led by the First Division Association) repeatedly attempted to have a Code of Ethics accepted by the government. Among other things, such a Code would set out the circumstances in which sanctions could appropriately be used against officials as opposed to ministers. The Thatcher government refused to acknowledge the need for such a document, and merely issued a 'Note of Guidance on the Duties and Responsibilities of Civil Servants in Relation to Ministers', in the name of the Permanent Head of the Civil Service, Sir Robert Armstrong. The implications of this are discussed in the next section. The behaviour and treatment of information officers during the Westland affair was one factor which led the Institution of Professional Civil Servants to formulate a Code specifically for this breed of civil servant. In May 1989 this Code was rejected by Bernard Ingham, the PM's Chief Press Secretary and Head of the Government Information Service. Of course, Ingham had himself been a leading figure in the Westland affair. He rejected the Code, and did not consider that it would be 'useful' to have a meeting with the union on this matter.[24]

3. Civil servants and 'the public interest': official secrecy versus open government

To whom are civil servants accountable? This is a key ethical question, and one which we have already encountered at earlier stages in our examination of the civil service. It has been shown that, in strict constitutional terms, officials are accountable only to their ministers and their departmental superiors. In this book, an attempt has been made to show that in practice (if not yet in constitutional theory) direct civil service accountability to Parliament has become increasingly significant.

What of the possibility of accountability to 'the people' or 'the public interest'?[25] In some democratic states there are statutes which exist to 'open up' the system of government, in the sense that ordinary citizens have legal rights of access to all government information not specifically designated as 'secret'. Thus, in countries such as Sweden, the United States, Australia and Canada, the onus is on the government to justify withholding information. This often places a clear, positive responsibility on civil servants in these states to aid those seeking access to official information.[26] For example, in the United States, since 1974 civil servants have been liable to be disciplined if they wrongly refuse to release information.

In Britain, the underlying assumption has been that government information is secret unless there is a specific declaration to the contrary. However, it is not difficult to envisage circumstances in which an official's conscience might lead him or her to invoke an ultimate accountability to the public interest. It could be said that there are three types of occasion during which a civil servant might wish to disclose official information in the public interest (note that the official might wish to do this by 'whistle-blowing' in an open fashion, or by leaking in a more anonymous manner. The use of the term 'leak' in this discussion is intended to cover both methods). Thus, we can view disclosures broadly in terms of those which aim to expose illegal acts; those which expose unconstitutional acts; and those which draw attention to, or fuel debate on, politically controversial issues.

Having said that there are circumstances in which civil servants may be tempted to disclose information in the public interest, it should immediately be added that the possibility of severe sanctions hangs over any official who succumbs to such temptation. The

CSPCS Code contains an entire section on the disclosure of official information. In addition to this internal form of discipline, there is the possibility of criminal proceedings being used. Until 1989 these were likely to stem from the use of the Official Secrets Acts of 1911 and 1920. The 'catch-all' Section 2 of the 1911 Act applied to any unauthorised disclosure of official information. In 1989, a new Official Secrets Act was placed on the statute book. The implications of this will be discussed in due course.

During the 1980s a series of celebrated cases brought into focus the whole concept of the civil service leak in the public interest. Before examining a few of these, let us briefly take the opportunity to point out that the principle of leaking, even for political reasons, has a respectable history. It would seem, on the surface at least, that officials who leak in order to draw attention to a matter of political controversy, or to add fuel to debate on such a matter, are in a particularly weak position. Cases where officials leak in order to expose instances of corrupt or unconstitutional conduct somehow attract an air of righteousness which is perhaps more difficult to associate with the politically motivated leak. However, we should remember that even those cases which have a basis in legal or constitutional issues can come, in time, to take on the characteristics of political controversy. In any case, even matters which are politically sensitive, but do not necessarily involve corruption or unconstitutional conduct, can provide instances where leaks are justifiable. The most famous such case occurred in the 1930s.

Much of the information which Winston Churchill used when attacking the defence policies of governments during those years was provided by Desmond Morton, head of the government's Industrial Intelligence Centre. Churchill later claimed that Morton had been given official permission to keep him informed by passing on secret information, but no evidence has ever been found to support this assertion. Furthermore, as Churchill's biographer pointed out, the government stood to gain nothing from conniving at the supply of politically sensitive information to this notable backbench critic. Indeed, they repeatedly attempted to discredit the figures on German rearmament which Churchill used.[27] The Morton leaks were specifically intended to fuel debate on this politically controversial issue: they did not aim to expose illegal or unconstitutional acts.

During the period of the Thatcher government there were spells when the flow of leaks from departments of state seemed to be without end. In August 1983 Sir Robert Armstrong sent a letter to each of the forty Whitehall Permanent Secretaries, in which he referred to the spate of leaked government documents which had appeared during the general election campaign in June of that year. He clearly blamed the civil service for these leaks, and asked every Permanent Secretary to be more vigilant. Before long, it became known that Scotland Yard's Serious Crimes Squad was at work in the Whitehall corridors. Early in 1984 two 'moles' were traced: Sarah Tisdall, a Grade 10 clerk working in the Foreign Secretary's office, and Ian Willmore, an Administration Trainee in the Department of Employment.[28]

In October 1983 Tisdall anonymously delivered documents to *The Guardian*. Among these was the Foreign Secretary's copy of a memorandum which had been sent by Defence Secretary Michael Heseltine to the Prime Minister. This contained details concerning the way in which the Defence Secretary proposed to handle the public and parliamentary announcements of the arrival of cruise missiles at the Greenham Common air base. *The Guardian* ran stories based on this information. Tisdall later claimed that she had leaked the documents for two reasons: a general disenchantment with government policies, and anger that Michael Heseltine seemed to her to be planning to evade his detailed accountability to Parliament on the issue of the missiles. After a legal struggle, the newspaper returned the key document to the government, Tisdall was identified as the source of the leak and charged under Section 2 of the Official Secrets Act. In March 1984 she was sentenced to six months imprisonment at the Old Bailey.

The Willmore case was less dramatic, but bore certain similarities to the Tisdall case. Like Tisdall, Willmore was generally disenchanted with government policies, especially those relating to the civil service. He also had a more specific reason for leaking, which was linked to what he saw as an instance of unconstitutional behaviour. Sarah Tisdall's immediate 'constitutional' reason for leaking seemed in retrospect to be somewhat shaky (since the Defence Secretary was going to appear in the Commons to answer questions about the arrival of cruise before giving his press conference at Greenham Common). However, Willmore's 'constitutional' reason seemed to be more substantial.

He had come across a document in the Department of Employment which contained an account of a meeting which had taken place between Michael Quinlan, who was about to become Permanent Secretary of the Department, and Sir John Donaldson, the Master of the Rolls. This account showed that the senior judge had made politically sensitive suggestions about the desirability of reforms in industrial relations law designed to restrict the right to strike. Willmore was angered by what he saw as the compromised position of a senior member of the judiciary. Donaldson was hearing controversial cases in the Court of Appeal relating to industrial disputes, and Willmore took the view that suggestions he had made in the course of the meeting with Quinlan were unconstitutional and unethical. Willmore sent a copy of the document to the magazine *Time Out*, and it was published at the end of November 1983.

The government could not prove that Willmore had leaked this document, but, in the course of an interview with a senior security adviser, he confessed that he was the 'mole', in return for a promise of immunity from prosecution. His resignation from the civil service was accepted early in 1984. In both the Tisdall and Willmore cases, documents were leaked because civil servants saw themselves as having a duty to the public interest which overrode their duty to the government of the day. This theme was to recur, in spectacular fashion, in what came to be known as the Ponting affair.

Clive Ponting, an Assistant Secretary in the Ministry of Defence, had become increasingly unhappy about the way senior ministers in his department were handling Parliament's attempts to get at the truth of the circumstances surrounding the sinking of the Argentine cruiser *General Belgrano* during the Falklands War in May 1982. By July 1984 Ponting was convinced that his political superiors (specifically the Secretary of State Michael Heseltine, and the Minister of State John Stanley) were taking steps to deliberately mislead MPs on the Foreign Affairs Select Committee. Ponting took this matter very seriously indeed. He concluded that, in this particular case, his constitutional duty to the state effectively placed him in a positive relationship of responsibility to the public via their parliamentary representatives.

All my instincts after fifteen years in the civil service told me that my loyalty was to ministers and the department. But then I realised that ministers had broken their side of the bargain in attempting to evade their responsibilities to Parliament. If they could just simply shrug off their duties, refuse to answer questions, give misleading answers or refuse to correct false statements to Parliament, how could there be any effective control over what the government did? In the end ministers had to be responsible to Parliament or the whole British constitutional system would break down. It never occurred to me to send the papers to the newspapers. This was a matter for Parliament.[29]

He decided to send a copy of the document which proved that his ministers were planning to deceive the select committee to Tam Dalyell. This Labour MP had been consistently misled on almost every occasion he had asked a question about the *General Belgrano*, and Ponting was convinced he would make appropriate use of the material. Ponting was speedily identified in the course of the MoD investigation which followed the leak. Initially, he was told by his official superiors that he would be allowed to resign from the civil service, but before this could happen, he was charged under Section 2 of the Official Secrets Act. At the end of his Old Bailey Trial in February 1985, Ponting was acquitted by the jury.

The prosecutions of Sarah Tisdall and Clive Ponting brought the already discredited Official Secrets Acts into further disrepute. The use of the catch-all Section 2 against Tisdall seemed akin to cracking a nut with a hammer. The refusal of the Ponting jury to follow the judge's virtual recommendation to convict said something about the ordinary citizen's contempt for this law. Furthermore, these cases, together with that of Ian Willmore, raised the whole question of how civil servants should act when confronted with a crisis of conscience.

A crisis of conscience had also affected another official involved in leaking a government document. As we have seen, in Colette Bowe's case the disclosure took place with ministerial approval. The Official Secrets Act was not to be wielded against this or any of the other civil servants (or ministers!) involved in the Westland leak. However, Bowe had experienced a genuine crisis of conscience regarding the furtive disclosure of the contents of a senior Law

Officer's letter (the Press Association was offered 'unattributable' extracts). What was an official to do in this position? She was torn between her duty to her official and ministerial superiors, on the one hand, and her duty to act responsibly in the public interest on the other.

Some thought had been given to this particular dilemma in the wake of the Ponting affair. As was noted in Chapter Four, the First Division Association and other civil service unions had come out in favour of an official code of ethics and an appeals procedure to put the minister–civil servant relationship on a slightly different footing.[30] Sir Douglas Wass, the former Permanent Secretary at the Treasury and Head of the Home Civil Service, suggested the establishment of independent appeals procedures designed to resolve the dilemma facing an official with a crisis of conscience. These would perhaps be based on a civil service 'Ombudsman' or an 'Inspector General'.[31]

For its part, the government continued to place great faith in the traditional procedures. Robert Armstrong, Cabinet Secretary and Head of the Civil Service at the time of the Tisdall, Willmore and Ponting affairs, was more or less obliged to offer a constructive statement which might help those officials who faced a dilemma when confronted with possibly illegal, unconstitutional or even simply politically controversial instructions from their superiors. However, his Note of Guidance on the Duties and Responsibilities of Civil Servants in Relation to Ministers (the 'Armstrong Memorandum'), simply reiterated constitutional facts.[32] To Armstrong, the matter was simple. Civil servants were accountable only to their superiors in the administrative hierarchy, and to ministers. If requested to participate in unscrupulous and possibly illegal activities, the conscientious official could not invoke any superior accountability to 'the people' or Parliament, but should consult a personnel officer or the Permanent Secretary of the department. As a last resort, the official could resign in protest.

The Armstrong Memorandum was bitterly attacked by, among others, Clive Ponting, who pointed out that,

> even if he does resign the civil servant cannot make public the reasons because he would still risk prosecution under the Official Secrets Act.[33]

Armstrong's guidance proved to be useless in Colette Bowe's case. She was unable to consult either her Principal Establishment Officer or her Permanent Secretary, in accordance with the Armstrong Memorandum, because these people could not be reached at the height of the crisis. Offered reassurance by her fellow conspirators, Bowe eventually felt able to go ahead with the leak.

To the end of his career, it seemed that Sir Robert Armstrong was quite unable to appreciate that in certain circumstances there might be a serious conflict between the duties of the civil servant, the requirements of a particular government, and the public interest. Like Margaret Thatcher, he seemed to associate the national interest with the interest of the party in government. Perhaps this helps to explain why he was prepared to adopt such a high profile during the *Spycatcher* affair in 1987. He willingly appeared in an Australian court setting out the government's highly controversial case for banning publication of this book written by Peter Wright, a former M15 agent, who gave details of various attempts by British Security Service officers to destabilise the Labour Governments of the 1960s and 1970s.[34] To many observers, inside and outside the civil service, Armstrong's defence of secrecy in this case was taking the civil servant's loyalty to the government of the day a step too far.

Supporters of the concept of a civil service duty to the 'public interest' traditionally placed a great deal of faith in reform of the Official Secrets Acts (especially repeal of the 1911 Act's 'catch-all' Section 2). As a major step towards opening up the machinery of government, it was argued that the correct reform could reconcile the obvious need for governments to expect loyalty from their permanent officials, with the equally obvious fact that occasions could arise in which the same officials might have to consider other loyalties.

Over the years, a number of drafts were put forward by would-be reformers from all parties. Repeal of Section 2 would allow former civil servants to 'blow the whistle' on illegal or unconstitutional activities without fear of prosecution, while new, more rational restrictions would cover the disclosure of information related to genuine matters of national security. A blanket contractual obligation towards the government would no longer follow civil servants to the grave. Officials who found themselves in the position of

Sarah Tisdall could be disciplined in accordance with the requirements of the CSPCS Code, rather than being treated as serious criminals. For reformers, the ideal was to create a significant measure of freedom for the 'whistle-blower' while reducing the punitive sanctions which could be brought against the malicious leaker (except when national security had been endangered).

When the long-awaited reform of the Official Secrets Act was caried out, it proved to be a severe disappointment to the idealists in all parties. The 1911 Act in particular had been torn apart by the events of the 1980s (only some of which were related to the themes we are considering). However, the 1989 Official Secrets Act was to retain most of the objectionable and flawed features of the old legislation, as well as introducing some new ones. The 1989 Act created a number of categories of information which would be covered by criminal sanctions against disclosure. As far as security and intelligence information was concerned, disclosure became an absolute offence, regardless of harm done. In four other categories (defence, international relations, information received confidentially from other governments or international bodies, and information useful to criminals) the prosecution had to establish that disclosure was harmful. Virtually all other official information remained protected by the threat of CSPCS Code sanctions. Furthermore, it became an offence for anyone, not only officials, to disclose information covered by the Act. Thus, publication of leaked documents became an offence for the first time. There was to be no 'public interest' defence: juries would be given no scope to decide whether a disclosure was designed to publicise unconstitutional or illegal, let alone politically contentious, actions. If the prosecution could show that 'harm' had been done by a disclosure, the leaker had no resort to the plea that such harm was the lesser of two evils (the greater being damage to the 'public interest').

Under the new Act, Sarah Tisdall would still have been prosecuted. Furthermore, *The Guardian* newspaper would also have been liable to prosecution in that case! Clive Ponting would have been unable to mount any meaningful defence of his actions. The relationship between the duties of civil servants and the 'public interest' seemed to be as obscure as ever.

6 Managerialism and 'Efficiency'

The need for efficient and effective management of the civil service as a whole, and of its component parts, has been a recurring theme in the history of this institution. It could be argued that every major investigation into the running of the civil service, from the Northcote-Trevelyan inquiry onwards, has been concerned to a greater or lesser extent with this need for sound management.

In Chapter 3 we argued that one of the key roles undertaken by middle and upper ranking civil servants is that of departmental manager. The practices and techniques of personnel, financial and resource management tend to change rapidly in response to new academic theories and the experience of managers, particularly those working in the private sector. In the period since the 1960s there has been an increasing expectation that civil service managers would assimilate and utilise private sector methods. The contrast between the supposedly dated and slipshod management of the civil service, and the sharp, efficient management to be found in certain areas of the private sector, has arguably been overstated. Nonetheless, it is this comparison which has provided the impetus for many of the managerial changes that have been introduced in the machinery of government.

In this chapter, an attempt will be made to set out what seem to be the most significant themes in the civil service managerial revolution. We will be concerned with both the 'macro' and the 'micro' aspects of management: with the general management of the civil service as a whole, and with some of the more detailed managerial issues confronting departments of state.

1. Plowden and Fulton: origins of the new managerialism
It would be quite wrong to suggest that the management of departments of state only came to be taken seriously in the 1960s. Indeed,

many officials found it difficult to hide their irritation with the suggestion that the civil service was being dragged, kicking and screaming, into the age of scientific management. One civil servant wrote in 1971 of 'The Great Management Hoax':

> The characteristic of the last few years is a growth of the mythology of management. There has been a deliberate and persistent propagation of the idea that management is a new conception in the civil service, and an attempt to persuade people, in and outside the service, that analytical procedures of a kind which have always held an important place at middle executive levels have now been introduced as a startling novelty from the top, and that this is about to produce a new golden age of efficiency.[1]

However, if management was not a 'new conception' for the civil service, what was new was the respect given to it and the emphasis placed upon it from the early 1960s by the occupants of Whitehall's top posts. The Plowden Report of 1961[2] and the Fulton Report of 1968[3] ushered in a new era in which governments would come to attach increasing importance to the application of modern management techniques. Management in government was given a much higher profile. In particular, key aspects of financial management (especially budgetary control systems, resource allocation and 'efficiency drives') were stressed.

In fact, Plowden did little more than set the agenda, in the broadest sense, for future discussion of certain complex aspects of management. This agenda would include:

> the cost-consciousness of staff at all levels; the provision of special skills and services (scientific, statistical, accountancy O and M, etc.) for handling particular problems, and the awareness and effectiveness with which these are used; the training and selection of men and women for posts at each level of responsibility.[4]

A fundamental refrain in the Plowden Report was that too many senior officials spent too much time on one aspect of their role responsibility, the provision of policy advice, at the expense of other aspects, especially management of their departments.

With the assistance of a management consultancy group, Fulton examined the theory and practice of management in government in much greater detail. The recommendations which emerged dealt both with the central management of the civil service (this was to become the responsibility of a new Civil Service Department, which absorbed the functions of the Pay and Management side of the Treasury) and with the internal workings of departments (management services units were to be established and the principles of accountable management applied, while some departmental activities were to be 'hived off' to new agencies). Additionally, managerial change was to be brought about through the influx of new personnel, stemming from reforms in recruitment procedures.

The fortunes of Fulton have been well charted, and the reasons for the application and non-application of the wide-ranging recommendations have been examined in great detail.[5] For example, the reforms in recruitment procedures never materialised in the way Fulton would have hoped. Fulton had argued that the civil service would be best equipped for the challenges of the late twentieth century if its senior figures were not Arts graduates drawn disproportionately from the universities of Oxford and Cambridge. Instead, more scientists, technologists, accountants, indeed specialists of any description, were to be recruited in larger numbers from other universities and the polytechnics.

Despite modifications in recruitment methods, successful candidates for administration traineeships (the first step towards a career in the upper reaches of the civil service) continued to come predominantly from the ranks of the Oxbridge Arts graduates. In 1986, for instance, 387 (16 per cent) Oxbridge and 2,030 (84 per cent) non-Oxbridge candidates took the initial qualifying test. However, of those who passed the test and were subsequently successful at the Final Selection Board, 54 (54.5 per cent) were Oxbridge candidates and 45 (45.5 per cent) non-Oxbridge. Arts and Social Science graduates continued to be more likely to apply for this competition, and relatively more likely to succeed.[6]

Explanations for the continued dominance of the Oxbridge Arts graduates are varied. Are these people just naturally superior to those graduating from other universities and the polytechnics? Is it important that the qualifying tests and the Final Selection Board procedures (interviews, role-playing, group activities) are, in large measure, devised by successful Oxbridge Arts graduates of the past, who may, consciously or unconsciously, seek to recruit people in their own image? Does it all matter anyway, provided the civil service continues to recruit people who can perform effectively in the top posts?

Whatever view one takes, it cannot be denied that this particular Fulton objective remains far from realisation. Many of the other Fulton proposals were implemented more successfully, but usually in a rather piecemeal fashion. Nonetheless, the Fulton Report served as a catalyst, sparking off a detailed debate about key issues in the management of the civil service.

2. The rise and fall of the 'Quiet Revolution'

As Leader of the Opposition in the late 1960s Edward Heath planned what came to be known as a 'Quiet Revolution' which had the objective of overhauling the machinery of government by introducing major managerial reforms. Heath was advised by a 'Businessmen's Team' headed by Richard Meyjes from Shell, and including Derek Rayner from Marks and Spencer. After the Conservatives' election victory on 1970, members of this team began a two-year sabbatical in government, courtesy of their employers. Heath's businessmen were the driving forces behind many specific aspects of the 'Quiet Revolution'. His broad aims were to:

- restructure the government machine by creating a smaller number of large departments of state;
- institute a new, rational system of policy analysis and review;
- encourage the adoption of private sector managerial techniques (such as the accountable management schemes favoured by Fulton) throughout the civil service. A key role was allocated to the Civil Service College in this respect. Set up in 1970, in the wake of the Fulton Report, it provided in-service training courses and developed a research facility;
- use the Civil Service Department as a 'battering ram of change' which could overcome the managerial conservatism of the Treasury;
- create a new 'think tank' which would offer Cabinet ministers strategic policy advice;
- 'hive off' blocks of work from existing departments into new agencies.

The 'think tank' (Central Policy Review Staff) was discussed in Chapter 3. The topic of 'hiving off' will be considered in the final chapter. Our concern here will be to summarise the impact of the other aspects of Heath's 'Quiet Revolution' in civil service management.

The creation of new super-departments, partly as a means of streamlining and rationalising civil service management, had its modern origins in Harold Wilson's experiments of the late 1960s (for example, the creation of the Department of Health and Social Security in 1968). However, the concept of departmental 'giantism' was enshrined in a White Paper issued by the new Conservative government in October 1970. 'The Reorganisation of Central Government' (Cmnd 4506), dealt with a whole range of structural and strategic issues, and set the scene for the development of 'giantism' as a principle of organisation and management in government. The White Paper reiterated the Haldane Report of 1918 by identifying a need

> To improve the framework within which public policy is formulated by matching the field of responsibility of government departments to coherent fields of policy and administration.[7]

In the House of Commons debate on the White Paper,[8] questions were asked about the theory and assumptions of the new emphasis on super-departments. One MP in particular (William Rodgers) argued against the creation of fewer, larger departments, precisely because this would lead to greater importance being attached to the managerial as opposed to the policy aspects of senior civil servants' role responsibilities.

In practice, the experience of senior civil servants in the giant departments (such as the Departments of the Environment, Health and Social Security, Trade and Industry, and the Ministry of Technology) showed that giantism in itself did not bring about substantial changes to the nature of their daily work. Nonetheless, some senior officials later testified to the fact that they had become marginally more involved with departmental management than in the past. Sir Richard Clarke, the first Permanent Secretary of the Ministry of Technology, noted that

'The tasks of Permanent Secretaries change, with more emphasis on management and less on the details of policy .... [9] Sir Patrick

Nairne, who was Permanent Secretary at the Department of Health and Social Security between 1975 and 1981, attempted to quantify the increased emphasis on management:

> ... I was always conscious of a tension within the Department between, on the one hand, the need to do better in pursuing policy objectives ... and on the other hand, the current and exacting demand for better management supervision and greater managerial skills .... While I could never risk taking my eye off the ball of policy, I could never devote less than a third of my time to the tasks of management.[10]

Even before the end of the Heath administration, the pure doctrine of giantism, as seen in Cmnd 4506, was diluted. Some autonomous departments were created or recreated from the bowels of the giants. The DTI suffered two blows against its giant structure before the end of the Heath administration. In August 1972, an additional Cabinet minister was allocated to the department, and in January 1974, as a response to the oil crisis, a new Department of Energy emerged. The break-up of the DTI was to continue under the Wilson Government with a Department of Prices and Consumer Affairs, and separate Departments of Trade and of Industry being floated off. Meanwhile, over at the DoE, the Department of Transport reemerged. The Ministry of Overseas Development also resurfaced from the Foreign and Commonwealth Office.

Of course, the trend was not totally in one direction. In the constant redrawing of the Whitehall map some smaller departments returned to the folds of the giants. For example, the return of the Conservatives in 1979 saw the reabsorption of the Department of Prices and Consumer Protection into the Department of Trade, and of the Ministry of Overseas Development into the FCO. The Departments of Trade and Industry were to be amalgamated again in 1983. However, the general tendency after the early 1970s was for a relative decline in the total number of departments and an increase in the importance of a few giants.

As well as setting the scene for departmental restructuring, the 1970 White Paper, Cmnd 4506, also signalled the initiation of a series of Whitehall experiments with private sector managerial techniques. The Fulton Report's praise for the type of accountable management found in American business corporations was echoed in Cmnd 4506. Accountable management involved setting up distinct units within departments. In these units, 'outputs' would be measured against 'inputs' (including finance), and the perform- ance of civil servants could be measured. Where it was difficult to measure the performance of individual officials in terms of 'outputs', the concept of Management by Objectives (MbO) could be applied. This involved establishing a programme of objectives through a process of consultation between branch heads, or 'line managers', and their subordinates. The objectives would be set in an order of priority, with agreement on the precise dates for their achievement.

The experiments with accountable management in general, and MbO in particular, operated in a rather sporadic fashion. By 1974, the peak year, the Civil Service Department was running 45 MbO projects throughout Whitehall.[11] However, the com- plexities of MbO, coupled with a degree of staff resistance, ensured that this, and other strains of accountable management, went into decline over the next five years. An additional factor was un- doubtedly the belief on the part of some key figures in the post- 1974 Labour governments that business-oriented schemes were somewhat alien to the world of government.

At the same time as these experiments with accountable management systems were being set up, another, more specialised concept borrowed from the world of American business was also on trial in Whitehall. The 1970 White Paper, Cmnd 4506, proposed the adoption of a rational planning scheme which, it was believed, could operate within the framework of the British civil service. In brief, Programme Analysis and Review (PAR) was designed to evaluate departmental programmes by examining the priorities which underpinned them, and comparing these with other, perhaps contradictory principles operating elsewhere in the government machine. It was believed that PAR would allow ministers and their senior departmental officials to make rational choices about the components of their departmental programmes. PARs were to be conducted under the auspices of the Civil Service Department (later the Treasury) and the Central Policy Review Staff. Ideally, PARs would have become effective tools in the hands of a new breed of civil service managers. In practice, technical, administrative, political and economic factors combined to destroy the experiment:

> in the departments most of the attraction of a 'new style of government' became a thing of the past. With regard to PAR, the original distaste that some departments had for the exercise turned to disillusionment and, with pay-offs seen as minimal, PAR began a rapid move down the administrative priority list so that by 1977 it existed more in form than substance. Eventually, in 1979, the quick thrust of a dagger in HM Treasury laid it to rest.[12]

Some of the components of Edward Heath's 'Quiet Revolution' were barely recognisable by the time he left Downing Street in 1974. The failure of his attempt to transform civil service management was epitomised by the plight of the Civil Service Department. This had been set up in the immediate aftermath of the Fulton Report, and was initially presented as the 'battering ram of change'. However, the CSD gradually lost its grip over the various managerial experiments it was meant to be overseeing. It had been resented from the outset by those in the Treasury who had jealously guarded that institution's supremacy in the sphere of service-wide affairs such as personnel and manpower. Critics of the CSD were quick to point out that it was losing its very reason for existing as most of the Fulton proposals were gradually diluted or quietly dropped. However, its supporters, including the civil service unions, saw the CSD as a potentially vital bulwark against Treasury dominance and enforced cuts in manpower. The CSD limped through the latter part of the 1970s amidst debates about its future.

During the first two years of the Thatcher administration, the CSD seemed to exist on a knife-edge. The Cabinet Secretary, Sir Robert Armstrong, the Prime Minister's efficiency adviser Derek Rayner and his associates, all argued for a Treasury-CSD merger as a means of cutting civil service manpower and sharpening the quest for greater efficiency in the Whitehall departments. However, the Chancellor of the Exchequer, Sir Geoffrey Howe, did not welcome the additional pressures which a merger would bring to him and his team of ministers, while Sir Ian Bancroft, the Permanent Secretary of the CSD (and Head of the Civil Service) stoutly defended his department.

Nemesis awaited the CSD in 1981. In January of that year, the government announced its commitment to allocating the CSD a leading role in the modernisation of the civil service.[13] However, the Prime Minister's obvious distaste for the CSD's handling of the major industrial dispute in the civil service during the summer stiffened her resolve, and in November the 'battering ram of change' was dismantled. Sir Ian Bancroft and his deputy, Sir John Herbecq, were effectively pushed into early retirement, and the headship of the civil service was allocated jointly to the Cabinet Secretary, Sir Robert Armstrong and the Permanent Secretary to the Treasury, Sir Douglas Wass. CSD staff and functions were dispersed to the Treasury (manpower and remuneration) and a new Management and Personnel Office, located in the Cabinet Office. In August 1987, the MPO was disbanded, with its pay and conditions of service functions transferred to the Treasury and the residual management, recruitment, training and personnel functions going to a new Office of the Minister for the Civil Service within the Cabinet Office.

Even before the demise of the CSD, it had become clear that a new Treasury–Downing Street axis had been forged in the realm of civil service management. At the Downing Street end, the new driving force in the bid for managerial efficiency was the Prime Minister's Efficiency Unit, headed by one of the survivors from the early days of Heath's 'Quiet Revolution', Derek Rayner.

3. 'Raynerism': the quest for 'efficiency'

Margaret Thatcher's bid to transform the management of the civil service was motivated by her personal distaste for traditional Whitehall attitudes, and by her belief that the public sector as a whole needed to become 'leaner and fitter'. Financial savings were clearly to be a major objective of this attempt. The new buzz-words were to be 'efficiency' and 'value for money'.

Thatcher's antipathy towards the civil service stemmed partly from her experience as Secretary of State for Education and Science in the Heath government between 1970 and 1974. It was fuelled, while she was Leader of the Opposition, by her reading of Leslie Chapman's book, *Your Disobedient Servant*.[14] Chapman, a retired civil servant, painted a bleak picture of official resistance to sharper financial management. On becoming Prime Minister, Thatcher appointed Derek Rayner as her special adviser on efficiency. In addition to pioneering new managerial systems with Marks and Spencer (a firm which, to the PM, epitomised private sector efficiency), Rayner had considerable experience of Whitehall as a result of his work in the Heath government (he had been based in the MoD between 1970 and 1972). The Efficiency Unit was based in the Prime Minister's Private Office, and this was one indication of the importance attached to Rayner's work by the Prime Minister. The fact that Rayner had the complete confidence of the Premier gave him considerable clout.

The Unit contained a small group of civil servants who were seconded from Whitehall departments, as well as one or two consultants from the private sector. In total, the Efficiency Unit was usually staffed by about six people. 'Rayner's raiders', as they came to be known, coordinated the scrutinies, which operated in the following fashion:

- each department was required to select one of its young Principals as its own scrutineer. This official would liaise with the Efficiency Unit in Number 10 Downing Street;
- an area of departmental activity was selected for analysis;
- the scrutineer from the department involved was set loose on the day to day task of analysis, seeking to identify all opportunities for savings or increased effectiveness;
- within a period of 90 days reports were to be written, containing proposed solutions for any problems identified;
- the reports were sent directly to the department's Secretary of State, and to Derek Rayner, with no scope for intervention by senior civil servants;
- with the department's agreement and cooperation, work would begin on implementing the solutions within one year of the scrutiny starting.

Rayner's objective was to ensure that the findings of these scrutinies could be used to promote lasting reforms in management procedures throughout the civil service.

Which types of departmental activity were selected for Rayner scrutinies? An extremely wide range of activities! In order to offer a flavour of Raynerism, let us briefly mention a few of the more famous scrutinies. The most commonly cited example of a scrutiny relates to the rather absurd case of the government research rat. In

1982 Rayner's scrutineers discovered that Ministry of Agriculture research scientists were breeding their own rodents at £30 a time, while commercial laboratories were selling such creatures for £2. The previous year, an investigation into the Home Office's Forensic Science Service revealed that 34 per cent of cases handled by the Service contributed little or nothing to police investigations. In 1982, inefficiencies in the operation of the Passport Office were uncovered. These led to unacceptable delays for applicants. The inefficiencies were largely attributed to the location of this body within the Foreign and Commonwealth Office rather than in the Home Office, and to the use of an outmoded computer system. An examination of the system for supplying food to the armed forces unearthed extraordinary examples of waste and inefficiency:

> ... warehouses full of food that was stored for years, three separate distribution organisations, and nobody in charge of the system. It even took two months to answer a basic question such as the cost of running the system.[15]

The young MoD scrutineer who conducted this investigation was invited to present his findings to an enthusiastic Prime Minister and her Cabinet. He was later awarded an OBE for his efforts. His name was Clive Ponting. Ironically, Ponting found that a combination of military obstructionism (caused by rivalries between the three branches of the armed forces) and ministerial indifference resulted in the abandonment of his proposed reforms.

This was to be one of the problems with Rayner's scrutinies. There would very often be a significant gap between the potential savings identified and the achievements realised. Sometimes the scrutineers simply exaggerated the potential for savings. Political factors could intervene too, as happened in the attempt to reform the arrangements for paying social security benefits. A 1981 scrutiny concluded that it was inefficient to pay these benefits through post office order books, at a time when most people had bank accounts. Automatic monthly payments directly into bank accounts would have reduced DHSS administrative costs by £66 million each year. When the proposals became known, protests led by sub-postmasters, pensioners' organisations, trade unions and MPs from rural constituencies (where the role of sub-post offices was vital) ensured that the reform was diluted. The proposals were eventually introduced in a more limited form, producing savings of £29 million a year. There was a difference between Rayner's rhetoric about 'efficiency' and 'savings' and the reality. Nonetheless, it cannot be denied that savings were made.

When Rayner returned to Marks and Spencer in 1983 (as Sir Derek, soon to be Lord Rayner) 155 scrutinies had been carried out, identifying potential savings of £421 million a year. It was estimated that the annual savings actually achieved were in the region of £300 million.[16] Rayner's successors were Sir Robin Ibbs (formerly executive director at ICI) and, from 1988, Sir Angus Fraser (a civil servant who had chaired the Customs and Excise Board until 1987). The programme of scrutinies which had come to be known as Raynerism continued under these men.

There would appear to be two broad views about the scrutinies. The first sees Raynerism as a rather blinkered approach to efficiency, which stressed financial savings at the expense of standards in the provision of services.[17] While few would deny that the scrutinies identified some ridiculous examples of overspending and inefficiency, the civil service unions became increasingly suspicious about the links between Raynerism and Thatcherism. The Efficiency Unit's proposals fitted logically into the Prime Minister's drive to reduce the size of the civil service. As the total number of officials fell from over 730,000 in 1979 to under 570,000 in 1989, it was not surprising that many civil servants should view the work of the Efficiency Unit with some unease. Clive Ponting, no supporter of Whitehall traditionalism and an enthusiast for some aspects of Raynerism, expressed his doubts about the prevailing definition of 'efficiency' in terms of short-term financial savings and fewer civil servants:

After nine years of Thatcherism the civil service could certainly be said to have emerged leaner, but not necessarily fitter; it has been not so much slimmed down as hacked at around the edges.[18]

Ponting believed that senior civil servants had neutralised the most useful aspects of Raynerism, while the Prime Minister had enthusiastically supported most of the negative implications of the drive for 'efficiency'.

The second general view is more positive, and sees Raynerism as a largely successful attempt to begin the transformation of civil service management. The National Audit Office investigated the impact of the scrutiny programme between 1979 and 1983. With only a few marginal reservations, the NAO concluded that the first phase of Raynerism had demonstrated the usefulness of scrutinies as a high level management technique.[19] A similar review by the House of Commons Public Accounts Committee also gave Raynerism a clean bill of health.[20] Of course, the PAC and the NAO would themselves act in a fashion which built upon the initiatives of the scrutinies. Increasingly, the system of audit spearheaded by these bodies would focus on applying tests of 'value for money' as well as simply gauging the accuracy of the departmental accounts.

Praise for the scrutiny programme was also forthcoming from the academics who conducted the most detailed analysis of its impact. Les Metcalfe and Sue Richards saw the work of the Efficiency Unit as much more than an exercise in short-term cuts. They argued that the new approach had

> broken through the barriers that previous initiatives ... failed to surmount because circumstances were created that gave top management in government departments no alternative but to act and provided them with a methodology for doing so.[21]

4. Rayner's legacies: MINIS and the FMI

As Rayner had intended, his programme of departmental scrutinies sparked off some managerial reforms which came to be applied throughout the civil service. A major example of this has been the development of management information systems. On becoming Secretary of State for the Environment in 1979, Michael Heseltine found that this huge department had no proper system for providing ministers and senior civil servants with data which he considered was vital if they were to make rational decisions. Heseltine had a personal interest in the application of private sector management techniques to government, and he asked Rayner to conduct one of the first scrutinies in the Department of the Environment.

As a result of this scrutiny, early in 1980 Heseltine set up a Management Information System for Ministers (MINIS) in his department. This was designed to allow ministers and senior civil servants to understand more about the cost and effectiveness of departmental programmes. 'Line managers' were to be more clearly identified, and they would be given more responsibility for running their operations in line with ministerial objectives. The system operated as follows:

- a MINIS Unit was established to oversee and coordinate the scheme;
- Under Secretaries were put in charge of the huge department's directorates. They compiled reports on the activities, objectives, priorities and budgets of the directorates. These reports were sent to the MINIS Unit;
- a series of meetings took place between the Under Secretaries, more senior officials and ministers. In these, the reports were discussed and proposals for change agreed;
- the proposals were implemented;
- at the start of the next MINIS round, there would be a review of progress made on implementing the last set of proposals for change.

As MINIS developed in the DoE, its implications for ministers and their senior civil servants became clear. The existing management systems in departments of state (staff inspections, organisation and methods study, internal audit, and so on) required no personal ministerial involvement, and minimal participation by senior officials. The Rayner scrutinies did usually bring short-term involvement both for ministers and their Permanent Secretaries. MINIS, however, necessitated a considerable managerial role for Under Secretaries as heads of departmental directorates, a coordinating role for Deputy Secretaries and top level managerial briefings involving Permanent Secretaries and ministers. Once the system became established in the DoE, the involvement of ministers and their senior officials increased.

The most important organizational change has probably been the increased role of the Permanent Secretary and other senior management in the DoE. For MINIS 1 and 2, the Permanent Secretary and other senior officials just took part in the Secretary of State's meetings with directorates, but in MINIS 3, a preliminary set of meetings was taken by the senior management of the department, headed by the Permanent Secretary to enable more ground to be covered and so that the Secretary of State knew the views of senior management. It was then up to the Secretary of State to decide whether he would see the directorate, and in practice for MINIS 3 he has mostly decided to do so.[22]

Heseltine was convinced that MINIS enabled ministers and senior civil servants to ensure that departmental resources were being used in ways which reflected policy priorities.

On becoming Secretary of State for Defence in 1983, Heseltine set up a MINIS in the MoD. By that time, steps had been taken to ensure that management information systems were used throughout Whitehall. Although supported by the Prime Minister, Heseltine had initially failed to convince his Cabinet colleagues that his particular form of managerialism had wider applications. However, in 1982 the House of Commons Treasury and Civil Service Select Committee offered support for Heseltine's ideas.[23] In responding to the Committee's report, the government committed itself to extending management information systems and, indeed, to launching a new Financial Management Initiative (FMI).

With the support of the Prime Minister and the cooperation of Derek Rayner, an offshoot of the Efficiency Unit drafted an outline for this initiative, which was launched in May 1982. A White Paper, published in September of that year, set out the objectives of the FMI.[24] These were refined and developed in subsequent documents.[25] The FMI was to be coordinated by a Financial Management Unit (later renamed the Joint Management Unit), run jointly by the Treasury and the Management and Personnel Office. The FMI obliged all departments to adopt an equivalent of Heseltine's MINIS to suit their own needs. The government made £35 million available for the new computer systems which would be required. Before long, the MINIS of the DoE and MoD were joined by the MAISY of the Treasury, the TRIDENT of the Department of Education and Science, the DEMIS of the Department of Energy, the MAXIS of the Department of Transport, and so on, across Whitehall.

The FMI involved more than the spread of management information systems, however. The Initiative required departments to make greater use of a whole range of financial management techniques, including:

- creating systems to distinguish between the management of

programme expenditure (i.e. spending on a department's services, policies) and the management of administrative expenditure;

- establishing cost centres within branches of departments, to allow for greater budgetary control, and the identification of accountable 'line managers'. These managers would have substantial budgetary power devolved to them;
- using more rational budgetary systems (i.e. systems which raise questions about the principles underpinning spending priorities);
- developing performance indicators and output measurements to assess success in achieving objectives;
- adopting more sophisticated tests for 'value for money'.

We must remember that the FMI was by no means the last episode in the story of managerialism. In 1987 Sir Robin Ibbs produced a document entitled 'The Next Steps', which was to have potentially significant consequences for traditional ideas about civil service management. Because this relates to the topic of agencies, it will be discussed in the next chapter.

To what extent can it be said that the Financial Management Initiative actually succeeded in transforming the management of civil service departments? The simple answer is probably the correct one: it is too early to say. Certainly, there have been some indications that the disciplines of management have taken root at higher levels of the civil service than was ever the case under previous experiments with managerialism. The staunch political backing of the Prime Minister has undoubtedly been a factor here. Furthermore, it seems clear that, in a general sense, while allowing for the difficulties in measuring such things, there have been improvements in standards of efficiency and productivity in government departments. However, the FMI was intended to be a rolling programme of change, which would develop in slightly different ways, and at different rates, in the various departments.

In this light, perhaps it is not surprising that certain aspects of the FMI seemed to have stalled. For example, the devolution of budgetary powers to cost centres within departments has been rather patchy, partly because this represents a challenge to the traditional supremacy of finance divisions within the Whitehall hierarchies. Similarly, the development of performance indicators and output measurements has been retarded in many areas of

departmental activity, mainly because of the costs and the theor-
etical difficulty involved in clearly defining acceptable standards of
'performance' and 'output'.

The closest observers of Whitehall have always stressed that
lasting change could only come about when the traditional 'culture'
of the civil service changed. This would involve giving much greater
emphasis to, and credit for, managerial skills in the upper reaches
of Whitehall. It would involve moving away from the historical
emphasis on the provision of policy advice. Above all, it would
involve rejecting what has been described as an 'impoverished
concept of management',[26] as a discipline with a limited application
in the public sector, and a relevance only for lower ranking officials.
Some critics would argue that the FMI could never totally succeed
in this respect because of the irrelevance of many of its specific
proposals to the task of management in government, and the fact
that it was 'a Trojan horse for a government bent on cutting the
public sector.'[27]

Even in the most favourable circumstances, fundamental cultural
change in a body such as the British civil service is unlikely to take
place over a period of ten or fifteen years. However, one of the
key factors which can serve to accelerate and entrench change of
this type, is sensitive handling of personnel matters. In this respect,
the new managerialism has been markedly lacking. It is to this
topic that we now turn.

5. *Appointments, training, promotion, personnel management*
One of the most important charges which can be laid against
Raynerism, the FMI, and indeed the whole spirit of managerialism
in the 1980s, is that too much emphasis was placed on financial
management, at the expense of personnel management. It can be
argued that reformers who fail to obtain and retain the support of
most ordinary employees will be destined to run into significant
problems.

One of the earliest supporters of the new managerialism had
stressed the importance of taking basic personnel issues seriously.
The first head of Margaret Thatcher's Downing Street Policy Unit
was Sir John Hoskyns. On leaving his post in 1982, he launched a
stinging attack on the approach to management in both the political
and the official reaches of British government.[28] As far as the civil

service was concerned, Hoskyns argued that the entire system of recruitment and training was flawed. The civil service had, he believed, 'its own self-serving objectives and ethos'[29] which acted against managerial change. In order to break this mould Hoskyns favoured a fundamental shift away from traditional civil service neutrality and permanency, and towards a political 'spoils system'.

His proposals envisaged the top ten or twenty officials in a department (including the Permanent Secretary) changing according to which party was in power. The political appointees would not be mere political hacks, but business people who had served the party for a time in opposition as preparation for running departments of state. Thus, talented business people could take career breaks with a party in opposition for four or five years, followed by a concentrated spell in government. The technical expertise of these new model, temporary civil servants would, Hoskyns believed, inject much needed spirit and enthusiasm into the management of departments.

Quite apart from the practical difficulties inherent in Hoskyns' proposals (how many business people would be prepared or able to take the lengthy 'sabbaticals' necessary to allow them to participate in government?) its rather heavy-handed critique of senior civil servants ensured that it would have a frosty reception in Whitehall. The Permanent Secretary to the Treasury and Joint Head of the Civil Service, Sir Douglas Wass, argued that the introduction of a 'spoils system' would lead to the sacrifice of a great deal of 'collective and historical knowledge' in the departments, and could discourage ambitious young people of ability from joining the service. A further problem was foreseen:

> There would be a major problem ... of ethics over business appointments when political advisers and managers left the service on a change in administration. We are rightly stringent at present over the conditions on which senior people can leave the service for industry.[30]

Sir Patrick Nairne, the former Permanent Secretary at the DHSS, also publicly questioned the feasibility of Hoskyns' proposals. He asked whether the special skills which business people might bring into Whitehall would compensate for their lack of knowledge of the machinery of government. He concluded that 'political business in a parliamentary democracy is different from industrial, commercial or managerial business in the private sector.'[31]

The Hoskyns affair was important in that it clearly signified to the civil service that some of those closest to the Prime Minister saw the personnel aspects of managerialism in a rather simplistic light (it was no secret that Hoskyns'.views were shared by other Thatcher advisers). In their eyes, the civil service was so far beyond repair that they favoured grafting a new breed of outsiders onto the existing structure, instead of refining the procedures for appointment and training within a permanent career service. Although Margaret Thatcher did not attempt to implement Hoskyns' ideas, there can be little doubt that these sowed fresh doubts about the true objectives of managerialism.

It was not necessary to support a Hoskyns-style managerial 'spoils system' in order to recognise that there were significant flaws in civil service recruitment and training procedures. As has already been noted, the Fulton Report's proposals for reform in these respects were largely ignored. By the early 1980s only limited attempts had been made to widen the recruitment net, increase mobility across and within the grades, secure promotion by merit at the middle and lower ranks of the service, and encourage greater contact with spheres of activity outside the civil service. As for training, despite the useful function performed by the Civil Service College,

> Perhaps the most prominent feature of the British tradition of civil service training is that there is not very much of it, at least in any formal sense.[32]

The Financial Management Initiative was up and running before the Prime Minister received the Cassels Report on personnel management in the civil service.[33] A 'Personnel Work Action Programme' was launched. This came to fruition by 1988 and 1989, by which time Whitehall departments were issuing glossy brochures describing (in the new jargon) their 'human resource management' schemes. This new emphasis on personnel matters was prompted in part by the realisation that the early phases of the FMI, coupled with repeated political attacks on the 'inefficiency', of the civil service, had damaged staff morale. Another factor was the shrinking labour market. If the civil service was to compete with other prospective employers in recruiting the dwindling numbers of school leavers as the twenty-first century approached, serious attempts had to be made to develop more attractive opportunities, particularly for those who found themselves in the middle ranks of the service.

A whole package of measures emerged, including:
- opportunities to attend courses in, and obtain qualifications from, the Civil Service College and external business schools;
- shadow schemes, designed to allow officials to gain experience as observers in industrial and commercial organisations;
- job swaps with industrial and commercial managers;
- regular personal performance reviews with departmental superiors, which went beyond bland 'chats' to focus on the extent to which annual objectives had been achieved;
- merit pay awards to reward individual effort and initiative.

Inevitably, the full implementation of these measures would take time, but there were positive signs of progress by the early 1990s.

In addition, there were increasing signs that attempts to inject new blood into the civil service (on more limited terms than Hoskyns had proposed!) were meeting with success. In 1984 a political storm blew up when Michael Heseltine appointed Peter Levene, his former special political adviser and the chairman of United Scientific Holdings (a defence contractor) as Chairman of Defence Procurement for the MoD.[34] This was the most significant and controversial example of a growing number of secondments to the top levels of the civil service, which challenged the traditional appointment procedures overseen by the Civil Service Commission (which operates the appointment system for senior posts in the service). Levene had been appointed with a salary of £95,000, twice the normal rate for this type of post, without reference to the Commission.

The Civil Service Commission (composed of officials) sought clarification of the rules surrounding the Levene appointment. At first, the Prime Minister claimed that he had simply been appointed on secondment from his firm, but when the legal basis of this was questioned, new rules for such appointments had to be formulated (in May 1986). Under these, departments could make appointments for up to five years to Under Secretary or above, only in line

with Civil Service Commission guidelines (these stated that individuals seconded should be the best qualified candidates available).

The idea of opening up the civil service to new blood, not through
politically motivated placings, but via 'legitimate' appointments
supervised by the Senior Appointments Selection Committee of
the Civil Service Commission, was supported by the House of
Commons select committee on the Treasury and Civil Service[35]
and the Royal Institute of Public Administration:

> only about two per cent of the members of the Senior Open
> Structure are 'outsiders' temporarily brought in to fill particular
> vacancies. Whitehall is too cautious in this respect. More could
> be done centrally to liaise with business, universities and the rest
> of the public sector to seek out talent. More civil service posts
> should be publicly advertised, and applications for them en-
> couraged from the existing civil service and from outside
> Whitehall .... [36]

Many of the issues raised in this chapter (including appointments), and more generally in this book, have been placed to the
fore by the emergence of new departmental agencies under the
'Next Steps' extension to the FMI. It is to these agencies that we
now turn our attention.

7 Beyond Whitehall

In the Introduction to this book, when some basic factual information was presented, it was pointed out that Whitehall represents the tip of a huge iceberg, or, more appropriately perhaps, the steering wheel of our machinery of government. Attention naturally focuses on Whitehall due to the central importance of such themes as the minister–civil servant relationship and the role of Parliament as a scrutineer of official activity. However, it is beyond Whitehall that most of the work of the civil service is carried out, and most officials operate at some distance from their departments' headquarters in central London.

In this chapter, an attempt will be made to examine two aspects of the world outside Whitehall. First, and quite briefly, the idea of dispersing posts, within the existing framework of departments, but outside London. Second, and at greater length due to the increasing importance of the concept, the development of 'hiving off' departmental functions and personnel, into agencies.

1. Dispersal of jobs

Three main factors have motivated governments to consider the advantages of dispersing civil service jobs to departmental outposts beyond Whitehall. These are: political, technological and managerial. The political factor was particularly significant in the mid-1970s, when job dispersal was placed on the agenda as a serious issue. In 1973, an official report by Sir Henry Hardman examined the issue of civil service job location.[1] The Hardman Report suggested that between 50,000 and 150,000 jobs, of a largely executive nature, could be transferred away from London.

The Labour Government which took office in February 1974 responded positively to the main thrust of the Hardman Report, while taking a more limited view of the number of jobs which could be dispersed. The government committed itself to the dispersal of 31,000 jobs. Political reasons were clearly important. The jobs were mainly to be relocated in areas of high unemployment, and (particularly in relation to Scotland) where a rise in political nationalism threatened electoral support for the government.

This dispersal programme ran into serious problems. Most significantly, the civil service trade unions opposed compulsory relocation and fought hard to limit the programme's impact. Furthermore, dispersal aroused little interest or enthusiasm in the Civil Service Department. Part of the political motivation was undermined as the nationalist threat receded in the late 1970s. As a result, only relatively small numbers of jobs were actually transferred out of London. Among the most significant examples was the transfer of 5,000 MoD jobs to Glasgow.

When the Conservatives returned to power in 1979, they swiftly revised the target for dispersal to 6,000 jobs. This was achieved in a piecemeal fashion over the next few years, with the transfer of relatively small numbers of officials, such as the 427 from the Overseas Development Administration who moved north to East Kilbride.

In the late 1980s, however, the theme of dispersal was given a fresh lease of life by technological and managerial factors. The information technology (IT) revolution had an impact on the civil service which was at least as significant as that felt in other major spheres of employment.[2] Government departments had been amongst the earliest users of basic computers for pension, benefit and tax systems in the 1950s. The technology developed apace, and the departments quickly became major utilisers of desk-top computers, telecommunications networks, fax machines and word processors in the 1980s. By the latter part of that decade, it was estimated that 15 per cent of all departmental running costs were being spent on IT.[3] The Department of Social Security was among the trailblazers. The computer system at its Newcastle-upon-Tyne Central Office is one of the largest in the world. As the 1990s dawned, the DSS was extending its system for electronic assessment and payment of benefits to all 500 of its local offices.

As well as minimising the need for routine clerical work, the IT revolution meant that fewer civil servants needed to be based in centralised departmental headquarters. More sophisticated communications links created fresh opportunities for the dispersal of jobs to regional and local offices. If this provided one incentive for job dispersal, a more general managerial factor provided another. Spiralling costs of London office rents and rates, coupled with the rising cost of living for middle and lower ranking civil servants obliged to work in the capital, gave a fresh lease of life to the dispersal debate. The stage was reached where some departments were accumulating substantial numbers of 'permanent' vacancies (500 in the MoD alone) due to the problems encountered in finding people prepared to work in central London on civil service salaries. This problem was becoming increasingly serious. In 1988 the Civil Service Commission informed candidates for Executive Officer posts that they should not apply unless they were prepared to work in London and the south-east. The number of applications fell by 10 per cent.[4] With the numbers of school-leavers and graduates due to fall in the 1990s, it was clear that more attractive working locations would be a factor as the civil service competed with other potential employers.

The civil service unions remained suspicious, fearing that job dispersal could be used by the government to break the system of national pay negotiations, and might lead to the introduction of regional pay scales (the existing scales provide for a relatively small London weighting allowance, but are otherwise uniform throughout the country). Nonetheless, the Thatcher government's belated conversion to dispersal led to a continuing flow of initiatives. In the autumn of 1989 it was announced that at least 1,100 Department of Employment officials were to be transferred to Runcorn and Sheffield, 2,200 Inland Revenue staff to various locations in the north of England, and 1,200 officials from the Department of Social Security to Lancashire. A further 650 DSS officials, together with 1,000 from the NHS management executive within the Department of Health, were to be relocated in Leeds. Other dispersal schemes were in the pipeline.

Much greater thought seemed to have been given to these plans (particularly the DSS and Department of Health relocations) than had been the case in the earlier dispersal programmes. Features of the new scheme included:

- consultation of staff (via Gallup Poll) regarding their preferred locations;
- travelling allowances for families wishing to have a look at houses and facilities in Leeds;
- lump sum payments of up to £8,750 offered as compensation for the loss of London weighting allowances;
- guaranteed selling prices offered for houses in London and the south-east;
- legal costs paid for those who wished to buy second homes in Leeds;
- salary advances (of up to 50 per cent of an annual salary) repayable over 10 years.

For some officials, family and other ties would be too strong for them to contemplate accepting this sort of package deal. Two out of every five civil servants polled in the London offices of the Departments of Social Security and Health stated that they would be unwilling to move under any circumstances.[5]

While it seems likely that some departments, such as the Treasury and the Cabinet Office, will continue to employ the great majority of their officials in Whitehall, it is clear that the dispersal trend will further diminish the relatively low proportions of civil servants who work in the MoD and the Departments of Social Security and Health (all under 10 per cent). By the early 1990s only approximately 20 per cent of all non-industrial civil servants continued to work in Whitehall. It was highly probable that this figure would be pushed downwards as the new waves of dispersal made their impact.

2. Changing ideas about government agencies

Job dispersal schemes have as their basic objective the internal reorganisation of traditional departments of state. The establishment of a government agency, on the other hand, will usually involve a more fundamental change in departmental structure. In order for an agency to be created, a whole sphere of departmental activity will normally be floated off to become a semi-autonomous organisation in its own right.

Discussions of agencies are often complicated by the use of confusing terminology. They are located in the world of 'quasi-government', where species and sub-species of organisation exist.

Thus, one might encounter the Quango ('Quasi-autonomous non-governmental organisation'), the Quago ('Quasi-autonomous governmental organisation'), or the Non-Departmental Public Body, to name but three! There are important distinguishing features between bodies in these categories. Some are genuine off shoots from government departments, staffed by civil servants, while others have only limited connections with government and are staffed by outsiders of various descriptions. However, analyses of the world of 'quasi-government' have not resulted in the development of watertight categories, while the terminology remains rather convoluted. In order to simplify matters for the purposes of our discussion, let us use the term 'government agency' to apply to a body which is associated with one or more departments of state, and is staffed, at least in part, by civil servants.

Agencies are not new components of the machinery of government. For example, the Crown Agents, whose mismanagement we touched upon in Chapter 5, were established in the middle of the nineteenth century as purchasers of goods in Britain for colonial governments. Government agencies were traditionally set up as bodies which were seen as most suitable for the execution of specific functions which needed minimal ministerial involvement, or as bodies which could channel outside advice into government departments. In some agencies, as we shall see, these executive and advisory functions were combined.

In 1968, as part of its wide-ranging prescription for change in the civil service, the Fulton Report[6] recommended radical restructuring of government departments and the 'hiving off' of some functions into new agencies. Fulton's recommendations in this, as in many other respects, were implemented in only a rather limited form. It was not until the 1970s that the most significant departmental agencies were set up. In the wake of the Heath government's 1970 White Paper, 'The Reorganisation of Central Government',[7] the Defence Procurement Executive was carved out of the Ministry of Defence, and the Property Services Agency out of the Department of the Environment. Each had substantial executive and advisory powers relating to the purchasing of equipment for the armed forces and government departments, respectively. The Property Services Agency was effectively the old Ministry of Works in a new form.

In January 1974, the Manpower Services Commission was set up as an agency 'hived off' from the Department of Employment. The 18,000 staff of the MSC initially lost their civil service status, but this was reintroduced in 1976. In typical agency fashion, the MSC was headed by a Chairman (appointed by the Secretary of State for Employment). Incidentally, the MSC was a major participant in the job dispersal programme of the early 1980s, when it moved its operations to Sheffield. As unemployment mounted in the late 1970s and early 1980s, the MSC's budget doubled,[8] and it began to run a series of special programmes (such as the £1 billion Youth Training Scheme) designed to ease unemployment and tackle special training needs. A series of high-profile Chairmen (Sir Richard O'Brien, David Young – later Lord Young – and Geoffrey Holland) oversaw the rise to prominence of this massive agency. In 1987, the MSC was renamed the Training Commission. Its staffing was halved, while the new Employment Secretary (Norman Fowler) restructured a number of the training schemes and transferred responsibility for running Job Centres back to the parent department.

The MSC was an agency which seemed to be close to the heart of Prime Minister Thatcher, particularly when the dynamic Young was at its head ('David never brings me problems, only solutions', was the Prime Minister's famous summary of Young's approach). However, in the early 1980s, agencies were singled out for particular attention as unnecessarily bureaucratic and costly areas of the public sector. Following publication of the Pliatzky Report on 'non-departmental public bodies' in 1980,[9] the government announced specific targets for abolition. By 1984 the Prime Minister was able to report that around 700 of these bodies (out of approximately 2,000) had been abolished or cut in size, producing total savings of £118 million each year. However, the practical reality of this great onslaught never matched the rhetoric of the early 1980s, and it soon became clear that the net reductions in the numbers of these bodies, and their staffs, were marginal. Total expenditure on agencies and associated non-departmental public bodies continued to rise (from over £6 billion in 1979 to over £9 billion in 1987),[10] as the Thatcher government, like others before it, recognised the very real political and administrative advantages of using agencies in certain spheres.

In addition to general executive and advisory functions these bodies can allow governments to distance themselves from certain sensitive issues, can be used to undermine or by-pass other institutions, and can provide ministers with a not insignificant source of patronage (since they have powers of appointment over many key posts in agencies). Indeed, far from attacking the concept of government by agency, as its third term began the Thatcher government committed itself to a significant expansion in the numbers and importance of such bodies.

3. Enter Sir Robin Ibbs

In 1983, Sir Robin Ibbs succeeded Sir Derek Rayner as head of the Prime Minister's Efficiency Unit. Ibbs oversaw the implementation of the Financial Management Initiative (see Chapter 6), but gradually became concerned about the long-term impact of the reforms in departmental management. He was convinced that major obstacles were blocking the path to more substantial and lasting improvements in efficiency.

At the beginning of November 1986, Ibbs set three members of the Efficiency Unit (Kate Jenkins, Karen Caines and Andrew Jackson) to work on a project with the following terms of reference:

- to assess the progress achieved in improving management in the civil service;
- to identify what measures have been successful in changing attitudes and practices;
- to identify the institutional, administrative, political and attitudinal obstacles to better management and efficiency that still remain;
- to report to the Prime Minister on what further measures should be taken.[11]

By March 1987, Ibbs's team had interviewed over 150 ministers and senior civil servants. They undertook field trips to regional and local offices of Whitehall departments and government agencies, as well as visiting a number of private sector organisations where major managerial changes had been introduced in recent years (for example, ICI and the Halifax Building Society). Formal meetings were held with the Council of Civil Service Unions. The team's report, 'Improving Management in Government: The Next Steps', was with the Prime Minister in the Spring of 1987. Two of the major themes of the report were the limited nature of the post-1979 achievements in Whitehall reform, and the need for radical managerial and constitutional change. Perhaps it was not surprising that Thatcher ordered such a sensitive document to be kept secret until the June general election was over!

The 'Next Steps' report asserted that the existing unified civil service provided an inappropriate organisational framework for the successful performance of its varied tasks:

> the Civil Service is too big and too diverse to manage as a single entity. With 600,000 employees it is an enormous organisation compared with any private sector company and most public sector organisations. A single organisation of this size which attempts to provide a detailed structure within which to carry out functions as diverse as driver licensing, fisheries protection, the catching of drug smugglers and the processing of Parliamentary Questions is bound to develop in a way which fits no single operation effectively.[12]

The report concluded that the obstacles to achieving long-term managerial changes in the departments of state could best be overcome through the establishment of new agencies:

> We recommend that 'agencies' be established to carry out the executive functions of government within a policy and resources framework set by a department .... We use the term 'agency' ... to describe any executive unit that delivers a service for government. ... In some instances very large blocks of work comprising virtually a whole department will be suitable to be managed in this way. In other instances, where the scale of activity is too small for an entirely separate organisation, it may be better to have one or even several smaller agencies within departments.[13]

Since the authors of the report estimated that 95 per cent of the civil service is concerned with the delivery of government services, it is clear that the creation of these new executive agencies would involve a fundamental challenge to the existing civil service. The Chief Executives of the new agencies would be given enough managerial freedom over recruitment, salaries and gradings to ensure that established civil service procedures and norms would be shattered. Indeed, the report made it clear that some of the agencies might be located outside the civil service itself. It was envisaged that the Chief Executives and their key underlings would become constitutionally accountable in a direct sense to Parliament, as well as to their ministers.[14] Such an arrangement would imply the need for the trend which we identified in Chapter 4 (relating to *de facto* civil service accountability to Parliament), to become entrenched in the constitution.

Ibbs and his colleagues recognised that the creation of their new model civil service would only be possible if there was total political commitment to the reform. The concept of a central, Whitehall-based civil service limited to providing a policy advice service and secretariat for ministers, coupled with a complex network of departmental agencies designed to deliver services efficiently, would not be realised without a clear demonstration of such commitment. Accordingly, the 'Next Steps' report recommended that a Permanent Secretary be designated as 'Project Manager' to ensure that the reform was implemented.[15] After the dust had settled from the 1987 general election campaign, and the implications of the report had been fully digested, the government began to frame its response to the Ibbs proposals. This response, and the government's plans for the 'Next Steps' programme, were made public in February 1988.

4. The 'Next Steps' programme

Close observers of the Whitehall scene detected signs of a serious debate taking place around the themes of the Ibbs report, long before it was published.

The Treasury (so it was plausibly rumoured) opposed the scheme because of its perceived implications for weakening central control of departmental expenditure and civil service pay; but some senior civil servants (for example, in the revenue departments) were said to welcome it as offering the prospect of greater autonomy. The civil service unions apparently had mixed feelings. Whatever the rights and wrongs of the proposals – and at this stage outsiders, including parliamentarians, had to rely upon press reports about something that was still, apparently, being hotly debated in the innermost circles of government – they were clearly of major potential significance.[16]

The rather limited nature of some of the government's initial plans for the creation of new executive agencies seemed to indicate that the Treasury had succeeded in diluting the Ibbs proposals.

On 18 February 1988, the day the 'Next Steps' report was published, the Prime Minister made a statement in the House of Commons, generally accepting the recommendations.[17] However, she made it clear that there were to be no constitutional changes in relation to accountability, and emphasised that the Treasury would retain ultimate control over budgetary, pay and manpower issues. There was to be a 'Project Manager', who would coordinate the implementation of the 'Next Steps' programme. He was named as Peter Kemp, formerly a Deputy Secretary in the Treasury, who was promoted to the post of second Permanent Secretary in the Office of the Minister of the Civil Service. This minister, Richard Luce, held a press conference following the Prime Minister's statement. At this, with Sir Robin Butler, the new Head of the Civil Service, at his side, Luce gave details of the first phase of the programme.

Twelve executive agencies were to be set up. In total, these employed around 70,000 civil servants. Critics of the government seized on the obvious gulf between these figures, and the numbers which had been mentioned in the Ibbs report. The fact that several of the first candidates for agency status, such as Her Majesty's Stationery Office and the Meteorological Office, already had some of the characteristics of agencies anyway, served to heighten suspicion that the thrust of the Ibbs proposals had been neutralised. However, it was noted that among the first twelve candidates was the Employment Service (including those civil servants who work in Job Centres), containing 35,000 officials.

Furthermore, after the initial announcement, the government updated and expanded the list of candidates for agency status: to 29 in July 1988, and to 40 in July 1989 (by which time 10 agencies had actually been established). As the programme rolled on, by April 1991, 36 agencies had been established, employing over 150,000 civil servants. Over 134,000 officials were working within 30 bodies which had been identified as candidates for agency status (see Appendix 3). By far the most significant in the latter category were the Social Security benefits staffs, totalling 68,000. Peter Kemp estimated that at least 75 per cent of all civil servants would be working in executive agencies before the end of the century.[18]

Before we examine some of the key issues surrounding the 'Next Steps' programme, let us attempt to answer a basic question: how is an executive agency set up? All government departments are encouraged to take a fresh look at their detailed programmes and activities, and to examine these objectively. Ultimately, a department might question whether a particular programme or activity really needs to be managed within the framework of the civil service at all, in which case privatisation might become a serious option. If, in any given case, a department decides that a particular programme or activity should continue to be managed by government, but outside the traditional departmental structure, the case for creating an agency could be examined. At this stage, the key questions would be:

- to what extent is there scope for real improvement in the management of the specific programme or activity under consideration?
- do ministers really need to be involved in the day-to-day running of the unit dealing with the particular programme or activity?
- is the unit large enough to justify a major change such as the creation of an agency?

If, having considered these issues, the department (meaning, effectively, the Secretary of State) is convinced that agency status is a serious option, a process of consultation is opened up. This involves representatives from the parent department, the potential agency, the Treasury, and the 'Next Steps' Unit. The latter is the group of twelve or so civil servants headed by Peter Kemp, and located in the Cabinet Office as part of the Office of the Minister for the Civil Service.

The consultations proceed to the point where a 'Framework Document' is drawn up for the new agency. This addresses issues such as the definition of the agency's tasks, the financial management systems to be adopted, the role and responsibilities of the Chief Executive, the relationship between the agency and its parent department, and the relationship between the agency and its 'customers' or 'contractors'. At this point, one of the civil servants from the 'Next Steps' Unit will assume responsibility for ushering the new agency towards its official launch. Each of the civil servants working under Peter Kemp is a young potential high-flyer, who, at any given time, will be responsible for overseeing the progress of five or six potential agencies towards their launch. The time which elapses between the initial consultations and the launching of a new executive agency will vary considerably, according to the size and complexity of the programme or activity involved.

5. Key issues surrounding the 'Next Steps' agencies

The theory and practice of new executive agencies raised a number of very serious issues concerning the functioning of the machinery of government. A considerable amount of academic and political debate soon developed around these issues, although it was clear that definitive answers to many important questions would not emerge until a wide selection of agencies had been operating for a number of years. To simplify matters, let us discuss the key issues, first in the realm of management, and then in the realm of politics (while recognising that there is a considerable degree of overlap between the two).

As far as the management of the agencies was concerned, the basic idea had been that ministers would appoint Chief Executives, who would then be given freedom to run the new bodies on a day-to-day basis, and would have some power over manpower ('hiring and firing') and pay. This apparently simple formula raised a number of questions. How, precisely, were the new Chief Executives to be selected? Would they come from the ranks of the career civil service or from other spheres? To what extent would a Chief Executive's powers to 'hire and fire' break with the traditional forms of civil service recruitment and conditions of service? Could officials working in agencies transfer to posts elsewhere in the civil service as their careers developed? Would the pay scales offered within executive agencies be different from those in the mainstream civil service?

Some answers (albeit tentative ones!) emerged for questions of this kind, during the early phases of the 'Next Steps' programme. Chief Executives were recruited by various means: internal selection either from within the parent department or on a service-wide basis, or external selection by means of an open competition following public advertisement of the vacancy. Ministers would decide which method was most appropriate, and have the final say in the appointments. For most of the first set of new agencies appointments were made from within the civil service, but there were some instances (for example, the Historical Royal Palaces executive agency) of outsiders being appointed. Where this course was followed, civil service pay scales applied (a significant test-case in August 1988 saw ministers obliged to accept that the advertisement for the post of Chief Executive of Her Majesty's Stationery Office could not offer a salary beyond the civil service norm).

While Chief Executives would have some powers over the appointment, payment and disciplining of their own staffs, these were initially to be exercised within existing civil service guidelines and standards. However, the government became particularly keen to see the agencies exploit to the full a range of pay and management 'flexibilities' which were gradually being made available to managers across the civil service.[19] The idea of greater 'flexibility' had been floated in 'Working Patterns', an internal government report written in 1987 by Dame Anne Mueller, second Permanent Secretary at the Treasury. This document envisaged a fundamental division in the civil service. Officials working at the level of the Open Structure (i.e. the Principal grade and above) would continue to enjoy most of the advantages of the traditional conditions of service and pay systems. In particular, they would have job security. Officials outside the Open Structure could, potentially, have their terms of employment and pay scales varied considerably.

As far as the agencies were concerned, the 'flexibilities' provided the chance for Chief Executives to develop particular packages of pay and conditions of service for their own employees. They would have powers to pursue a number of initiatives, including:

- offering limited-period appointments and short-term contracts, up to the the level of Under Secretary;
- offering special rates of pay for special appointments (provided an attempt to make a particular appointment on the normal pay-scale had been unsuccessful);
- paying special responsibility allowances, and bonuses to recognise exceptional performance;
- introducing a new grading structure below Principal level;
- developing a detailed staff appraisal scheme (within the framework of existing national agreements).

In operating such schemes, and managing the agencies generally, the Chief Executives were working within a financial framework set by their own ministers and the Treasury. Chief Executives proposed corporate plans, budgets, financial and personnel management strategies for their agencies, and these were subject to ministerial approval. At the end of 1989, however, there came a clear indication that the government was prepared to see executive agencies enter a new managerial phase. A White Paper, 'The Financing and Accountability of Next Steps Agencies'[20] looked towards the creation of greater freedom of manoeuvre for Chief Executives. They would have more power to transfer funds *within* their overall budgets without seeking Treasury approval, and to carry over excess funds from year to year. The profit motive would become a more important factor as the agencies moved into an era of greater commercialism. The Chief Executives of the future would be given 'competitive' salaries within fixed contracts, containing specific objectives, and they would be subject to pay penalties or even dismissal if they failed to deliver the goods! In its turn, this would imply the need for Chief Executives to make greater use of performance indicators within their own agencies, in order to meet their targets and achieve 'value for money'.

This raised the real prospect of a further erosion of traditional civil service pay schemes and conditions of service, through the emergence of diverse systems in the executive agencies. Furthermore, it seemed to challenge the very concept of a unified civil service, within which officials could be transferred (at least in theory) with reasonable ease. If grading systems, pay and conditions of service were to become significantly different in the growing number of executive agencies, the careers of officials in these agencies would inevitably become detached from those elsewhere in the service. If the civil service of the future was *predominantly* to take agency form, it seemed clear that its corporate character would have been broken completely.

It can only be assumed that some figures at the very top of the Whitehall hierarchy viewed developments of this kind with a considerable degree of suspicion. In 1988, in one of his first public pronouncements as Head of the Civil Service, Sir Robin Butler addressed the Institute of Personnel Management. In the traditional, 'coded' form, he warned the government about the dangers of tampering with the unity of the civil service.

> The unity of the civil service offers stability and a continuing corpus of tradition, knowledge and experience which is part of the infrastructure of democratic society.[21]

While welcoming the 'Next Steps' initiative generally, and praising the advent of more flexible pay systems and conditions of service, Butler strongly defended the traditional Whitley negotiating system for these matters.

This type of unease about the long-term impact of the agencies on the civil service clearly goes beyond a concern which is related to the issue of managerial strategies and style, into a concern which is linked to constitutional and political factors. One of the biggest political issues which hovered over the entire 'Next Steps' programme from the outset was that of privatisation. The Ibbs report itself had suggested that some agencies might find a more natural home outside the civil service, in the private sector. When setting out her government's initial plans for executive agencies, the Prime Minister stated that these would 'generally' remain within the civil service, but admitted that there was a possibility of privatisation in appropriate cases.

The civil service trade unions, opposition parties and those who had observed the stealthy progress of privatisation in other areas of the public sector viewed the 'Next Steps' programme with a degree of scepticism. It seemed, potentially at least, to be a stalking horse for the privatisation of large parts of the civil service. In September 1989 there came the first clear indication that agency status might be seen as something of a staging post on the road to the private sector. The Secretary of State for the Environment announced that the Property Services Agency, not one of the 'Next Steps' bodies, but a survivor from the 1970s experiments with 'hiving off', was to be privatised.

Of course, privatisation raises the whole question of accountability for the provision of former public services and programmes, and it takes us beyond the scope of our study. However, this difficult question also arises in relation to the establishment of the executive agencies.

It has already been noted that the Thatcher government's commitment to the concept of executive agencies did not extend to the point where the Ibbs report's proposal for a rethinking of the constitutional rules on accountability were accepted. Thus, in broad terms, the government adhered to the tradition of individual ministerial responsibility, and denied that there was a need for Chief Executives to be legally and constitutionally directly accountable to Parliament. An analogy was drawn between the minister-Chief Executive relationship and that between a minister and the Chairman of a nationalised industry. This was not a very happy comparison. The Chairmen of nationalised industries had never been civil servants, while the agency Chief Executives were. Furthermore, over the years a disreputable tendency had developed, whereby ministers interfered in the day-to-day running of nationalised industries while shielding themselves from effective parliamentary scrutiny by claiming that their roles in the running of these bodies were limited.

All too aware that genuine accountability for the operation of the agencies could become diluted, Parliament pressed its case. If ministers were no longer to be accountable for the detailed operation of what had been significant programmes and activities run by their own departments, some devices were needed in order to allow MPs to monitor these parts of the government machine.

In 1988, the Treasury and Civil Service select committee launched an inquiry into the 'Next Steps' proposals. While supporting the agency concept as a suitable development upon earlier managerial innovations, the committee concluded that the authors of the Ibbs report had not paid enough attention to the role of Parliament.[22] In this respect, two clear proposals were made by the committee. The first was that House of Commons select committees should have the power to summon Chief Executives before them, and the latter should be allowed to give evidence on their own behalf, rather than as the mere mouthpieces of ministers. Of course, this would have involved a fundamental change in the Osmotherly rules which govern the appearance of civil servants before select committees (see Chapter 4).[23]

The government refused to be moved on this matter. Chief Executives, like other civil servants, could be invited to appear before select committees, but ministers would retain the power to decide whether this was appropriate in any given case. The

Osmotherly rules were to remain. The second proposal put forward by the Treasury and Civil Service select committee related to the specific issue of financial accountability. In their evidence to the committee, Peter Kemp, the 'Next Steps Project Manager', and Sir Peter Middleton, Permanent Secretary to the Treasury, denied that there was any need for agency Chief Executives to be designated Accounting Officers.[24] They argued that Permanent Secretaries of parent departments should be required to appear before the Public Accounts Committee as Accounting Officer for the department and its agencies. The Treasury and Civil Service select committee disagreed, and proposed that Chief Executives should be directly accountable to the PAC for the finances of their agencies. The government modified its stance on this issue. In its response to the committee's report, published in November 1988,[25] the government agreed that the responsibility for being the Agency Accounting Officers should reside with the Chief Executives. They would appear before the PAC, accompanied by the departmental Permanent Secretaries.

The Treasury and Civil Service select committee continued to monitor the early operation of the new agencies, and published another major report in July 1990.[26] While generally welcoming most of the initial developments, the committee continued to sound warnings about the arrangements for agency accountability to Parliament. In particular, there seemed to be continuing problems with the theory that ministers could be fully accountable to Parliament for their departmental agencies, while Chief Executives remain in charge of operational matters. A Question from an MP is answered by the minister if it relates to a strategic matter, but those Questions related to individual cases or operational issues are passed on to the Chief Executive, who replies to the MP. The reply from a Chief Executive may be placed in the library of the House of Commons, at the MP's request. The select committee registered its concern at this procedure:

Replies from the Chief Executive, even if placed in the Library of the House, are not freely available to those outside the House, nor is it clear whether they would attract Parliamentary privilege in the same way as written answers published in the Official Report ... there is a danger that, despite the wholly laudable intention of making those responsible for carrying out the service fully accountable to Parliament, much information currently available to Parliament and public will no longer be readily accessible.[27]

The establishment of new executive agencies raises many issues, of which accountability is but one, which go to the core of the civil service itself. Within the 'Next Steps' programme many of the themes we have been seeking to examine in this book can be seen in microcosm. If the agencies develop along the lines envisaged by their creators, it is conceivable that the civil service of the twenty-first century will be virtually unrecognisable, even to those of us who observe and study it in the latter part of the twentieth century. Its overall size and shape, its detailed management and operation, could have changed fundamentally.

However, we should remember that, in the past, the evolution of the civil service has been affected by a wide range of variables which can be difficult, if not impossible, to predict. There can be nothing inevitable about any programme of reform. Party political control over the levers of power can shift, providing opportunities for new generations of 'mechanics' to tinker with the machinery of government. Senior civil servants also come and go, albeit normally over a longer timespan than the politicians, and they too adopt different approaches to the institution within which they work. External pressures and challenges can change strategic priorities and force governments to mould and remould the civil service accordingly. Bearing these points in mind, it seems fair to conclude that our examination of the civil service today can only be seen as a snapshot of a continuously evolving institution, taken during a period of remarkable activity.

Appendices

Appendix 1
Non-industrial civil service staff numbers by department (1 April 1989)

Department	Staff in Post
Agriculture, Fisheries and Food	9,572
Cabinet Office	1,609
Customs and Excise	26,416
Defence	88,710
Education and Science	2,474
Employment	54,463
Energy	1,036
Environment	33,497
Health	8,820
Social Security	83,262
HM Stationery Office	1,987
Home Office	37,691
Inland Revenue	67,035
Land Registry	10,524
Lord Chancellor's Department	10,896
National Savings	7,241
Ordnance Survey	2,552
Office of Population Censuses and Surveys	2,065
Scottish Office	9,421
Trade and Industry	12,366
Treasury	2,585
Welsh Office	2,087
Other departments	23,512
TOTAL	499,821

Source: Civil Service Statistics, 1988–89 (HMSO, 1990).

Appendix 2
Non-industrial civil service staff by selected occupational group
(1 April 1989)

Group	% of Total
Administration Group	44.5
Open Structure	4.1
Science Group	2.1
Professional and Technology Group	4.9
Secretarial Group	4.0
Home Office Prison Grades	4.4
Social Security Group	9.2
Other Groups and Grades	28.8

Source: Civil Service Statistics 1988–89 (HMSO, 1990)

Appendix 3
'Next Steps' Executive Agencies

Executive agencies established*

Building Research Establishment
Central Office of Information
Central Veterinary Laboratory
Civil Service College
Companies House
Department of Registers for Scotland
Driver and Vehicle Licensing Agency
Driving Standards Agency
Employment Service
Her Majesty's Stationery Office,
Historic Royal Palaces
Hydrographic Office
Information Technology Services Agency
Insolvency Service
Intervention Board for Agricultural Produce
Laboratory of the Government Chemist
Land Registry
Meteorological Office

National Physical Laboratory
National Weights and Measures Laboratory
National Resources Institute
Occupational Health Service
Ordnance Survey
Passport Office
Patent Office
Queen Elizabeth II Conference Centre
Radiocommunications Agency
Resettlement Agency
Royal Mint
Social Security Benefits Agency
Training and Employment Agency (N. Ireland)
Vehicle Certification Agency
Vehicle Inspectorate
Veterinary Medicines Directorate
Warren Spring Laboratory

Total staff employed: 150,670

Executive agency candidates announced

ADAS
Cadw
Central Science Laboratory
Central Statistical Office
Chessington Computer Centre
Child Support Agency
Civil Service Commission
Customs and Excise
Defence Accounts Organisation
Defence Research Agency
Estates Directorate (Dept of Health)
Farm and Countryside Service
Fisheries Enforcement
Forensic Science Service
Fuel Suppliers Branch
Historic Buildings and Monuments Directorate
Inland Revenue
Military Survey

Ordnance Survey
Planning Inspectorate
Pollution Inspectorate
Property Holdings
RAF Training
Rating Division
Royal Parks
Service Children's Schools
Social Security Contributions Agency
Social Security Operations
Valuation Office
Youth Treatment Service

Total staff employed: 134,890

* as at 1 April 1991.

Source: Office of the Minister for the Civil Service, HC Written Answers.

Notes and References

Chapter 1 Introduction

1. Figures given in this chapter are taken from *Civil Service Statistics 1988–89* (HMSO, 1990).

Chapter 2 Historical Development of the Civil Service

1. John Blair, 'The Anglo-Saxon period', in Kenneth O. Morgan, ed., *The Oxford History of Britain* (Oxford University Press, 1988), p. 112.
2. Peter Hennessy, *Whitehall* (Secker and Warburg, 1989), p. 20.
3. Henry Parris, *Constitutional Bureaucracy* (Allen and Unwin, 1969), p. 21.
4. 'Report on the Organisation of the Permanent Civil Service', Parliamentary Paper 1713, 1854.
5. Peter Hennessy, *op. cit.*, p. 42.
6. Arbuthnot's remarks came in the form of a response to the Treasury's request for comments from educationalists and civil servants, printed collectively as 'Reorganisation of the Civil Service', Parliamentary Paper 1870, 1854–55.
7. Royal Institute of Public Administration (RIPA), *Top Jobs In Whitehall. Appointments and Promotion in the Senior Civil Service* (RIPA, 1987), p. 14.
8. Peter Hennessy, *op. cit.*, p. 68.
9. Report of the Machinery of Government Committee, Cmnd 9230, 1918.
10. For a useful discussion of the 'Haldane Legacy' see Peter Hennessy, *op. cit.*, pp. 292–299.
11. John P. Mackintosh, *The British Cabinet* (Stevens and Sons, Third Edition, 1977), p. 475.
12. Richard A. Chapman, *Ethics In The British Civil Service* (Routledge, 1988), p. 30.

13. RIPA, *op. cit.*, p. 16.
14. Peter Hennessy, *op. cit.*, p. 87.
15. See Peter Hennessy, *op. cit.*, Chapter 3, and Peter Hennessy and Sir Douglas Hague, 'How Adolf Hitler reformed Whitehall', *Strathclyde Papers on Government and Politics*, Number 41, 1985.
16. Hennessy and Hague, *op. cit.*, p. 42.
17. Richard A. Chapman, *op. cit.*, pp. 9–10.
18. Clark Report, Cmnd 9176, 1953–54.
19. Exhaustive accounts of the affair can be found in I. F. Nicolson, *The Mystery of Crichel Down* (Clarendon, 1986) and John Griffith, 'Crichel Down. The most famous farm in British constitutional history', *Contemporary Record*, Volume 1, Number 1, Spring 1987.
20. For a particularly trenchant critique, see Thomas Balogh, 'The apotheosis of the dilettante: the Establishment of mandarins', in Hugh Thomas, ed., *Crisis in the Civil Service* (Anthony Blond, 1968).
21. Fulton Report, Cmnd 3638, 1968.
22. Peter Kellner and Lord Crowther-Hunt, *The Civil Servants. An Inquiry into Britain's Ruling Class* (Macdonald, 1980), p. 76.
23. James Report, HC 113, 1971–72.

Chapter 3   Civil Servants and Ministers

1. See the *Civil Service Pay and Conditions of Service Code* (Management and Personnel Office, August 1980).
2. *Memorandum on the Responsibilities of An Accounting Officer* (HM Treasury, November 1981).
3. Tony Benn, *Against The Tide. Diaries 1973–76* (Arrow, 1990), Chapter 3.
4. Clive Ponting, *Whitehall: Tragedy and Farce* (Sphere, 1986), p. 39.
5. See, for example, *The Guardian*, 13 February 1985.
6. Susan Crosland, *Tony Crosland* (Cape, 1982), p. 202.
7. Anthony Howard, *RAB. The Life of R. A. Butler* (Cape, 1987), p. 369.
8. Maurice Kogan (ed.), *The Politics of Education. Edward*

Boyle and Anthony Crosland in Conversation (Penguin, 1976), p. 98.

9. Susan Crosland, *op. cit.*, pp. 266–7.
10. See R.H.S. Crossman, *The Diaries of a Cabinet Minister* (Hamish Hamilton and Jonathan Cape, Vol. 1 1975, Vol. 2 1976, Vol. 3 1977).
11. Barbara Castle, *The Castle Diaries 1974–76* (Weidenfeld and Nicolson, 1980), p. 209.
12. *Ibid.*, p. 331.
13. Tony Benn, *Out of the Wilderness. Diaries 1963–67* (Arrow, 1987), pp. 194–5.
14. *Ibid.*, p. 209.
15. Material in this section draws on Robert Pyper, 'The doctrine of individual ministerial responsibility in British government: theory and practice in a new regime of parliamentary accountability', Ph.D thesis, University of Leicester, 1987.
16. Bruce Headey, *British Cabinet Ministers* (Allen and Unwin, 1974) p. 187.
17. See Tony Benn, *Arguments For Democracy* (Penguin, 1982), Chapter 3; Brian Sedgemore, *The Secret Constitution* (Hodder and Stoughton, 1980) and Peter Kellner and Lord Crowther-Hunt, *The Civil Servants. An Inquiry Into Britain's Ruling Class* (Macdonald, 1980).
18. For illustrations of this Thatcherite view of the civil service, see Hugo Young, *One of Us* (Pan, 1990), Chapter 9; and Peter Hennessy, *Whitehall* (Secker and Warburg, 1989), Chapter 15.
19. See, for example, Sir John Hoskyns, 'Whitehall and Westminster: an outsider's view', *Parliamentary Affairs,* Volume 36, 1983.
20. See *The Civil Service. Report of the Committee 1966–68* (Chairman, Lord Fulton), Cmnd 3638.
21. Pauline Neville-Jones, 'The continental *cabinet* system: the effects of transferring it to the United Kingdom', *The Political Quarterly*, Volume 54, 1983, p. 234.
22. See Christopher Pollitt, *Manipulating The Machine, Changing the Pattern of Ministerial Departments 1960–83* (Allen and Unwin, 1984).

23. See Tessa Blackstone: 'Helping ministers do a better job', *New Society*, 19 July 1979.

24. See Hugo Young, 'How Whitehall's mandarins tamed Labour's 38 special advisers', *The Sunday Times*, 19 September 1976.

25. See *The Economist*, 27 August 1983.

26. Seventh Report from the Treasury and Civil Service Committee, 'Civil Servants and Ministers: Duties and Responsibilities', HC 92 1985–86.

27. Hugo Young (1976), *op. cit.*

28. *Ibid.*

29. For accounts of the rise and fall of the CPRS, see Peter Hennessy, Susan Morrison and Richard Townsend, *Routine Punctuated By Orgies: The Central Policy Review Staff 1970–83* (Strathclyde Papers on Politics, No. 31, 1983) and William Plowden and Tessa Blackstone, *Inside the Think Tank* (Heinemann, 1988).

30. See *The Independent*, 30 January 1989 and *The Guardian*, 30 January 1989 and 1 February 1989.

31. In the form of two lectures, later published as 'Whitehall and Westminster: an outsider's view', *Parliamentary Affairs*, Volume 36, 1983, and 'Conservatism is not enough', *The Political Quarterly* , Volume 55, 1984. It is often forgotten that Hoskyns argued for a dramatic expansion in the appointment of 'outsiders' to ministerial posts as well as to the higher civil service.

32. Hoskyns, *op. cit.* (1984), p. 145.

33. See Robert Pyper, 'Whitehall in the 1980s: prescriptions and prospects', *Teaching Politics* , Volume 13, 1984, pp. 380–383.

34. Peter Hennessy, 'Mrs Thatchers's poodle? The civil service since 1979', *Contemporary Record* , Volume 2, Summer 1988. See also Gavin Drewry and Tony Butcher, *The Civil Service Today* (Basil Blackwell, 1988), pp. 169–170; 215–216.

35. Dr John Cunningham, quoted in Peter Hennessy, 'Why new masters could mean wholesale change', *The Independent*, 9 January 1989.

36. Peter Hennessy, *Whitehall* (Secker and Warburg, 1989).

37. Seventh Report from the Treasury and Civil Service Committee, HC 92 1985–86.

38. RIPA, *Top Jobs In Whitehall* (RIPA, 1987).

Chapter 4 Civil Servants and Parliament

1. A Permanent Secretary, quoted in Robert Pyper, 'The doctrine of individual ministerial responsibility in British Government: theory and practice in a new regime of parliamentary accountability', Ph.D. thesis, University of Leicester, 1987, p. 90.

2. Three MPs, all former ministers, quoted by Anthony King, *British Members of Parliament: A Self-Portrait* (Macmillan, 1974).

3. A Permanent Secretary, quoted in Robert Pyper, *op. cit.*, p. 10.

4. Sir Antony Part, former Permanent Secretary at the Department of Trade and Industry, quoted in Robert Pyper, *op. cit.*, p. 104.

5. Vilna Flegman, *Called To Account. The Public Accounts Committee of the House of Commons 1965–66 to 1977–78* (Gower, 1980).

6. Justice, *The Citizen and the Administration. The Redress of Grievances* (Stevens, 1961).

7. HC Deb 5s 666 1962–63 c1125–26.

8. HC Deb 5s 734 1966–67 c59.

9. Initially, the PCA had no power to investigate allegations of failings in the National Health Service, but in 1973 an additional office of Health Service Commissioner was created, and this has been held concurrently with the post of PCA by incumbents since then.

10. A Permanent Secretary, quoted in Robert Pyper, *op. cit.*, p. 172.

11. A Permanent Secretary, quoted in Robert Pyper, *op. cit.*, p. 173.

12. Roy Gregory, 'The Select Committee on the Parliamentary Commissioner for Administration 1967–1980', *Public Law*, Spring 1982, p. 56.

13. Standing Orders of the House of Commons, Public Business 1979, HC 266 1979–80 para 86A.

14. Cited by Geoffrey Lock, 'Resources and operations of Select Committees: a survey of statistics', in Gavin Drewry, ed., *The New Select Committees. A Study of the 1979 Reforms* (Clarendon, 1985), p. 330.

15. C. M. Regan, 'Anonymity in the British civil service: faceless-

ness diminished', *Parliamentary Affairs*, Volume 39, Number 4, October 1986, p. 430.

16. *Ibid.*, p. 431.

17. Select Committees, Memorandum of Guidance for Officials, CSD General Notice, Gen 80/38, 16 May 1980.

18. *Ibid.*, para 25.

19. *Ibid.*, paras 26 and 29.

20. Hugo Young and Anne Sloman, *No, Minister* (BBC, 1982), p. 65.

21. A Permanent Secretary, quoted in Robert Pyper, *op. cit.*, p. 159.

22. Frank Hooley MP, then Chairman of the Select Committee on Foreign Affairs, Sub-Committee on Overseas Development. Quoted in Robert Pyper, *op. cit.*, p. 159.

23. Sir Kenneth Couzens, former Permanent Secretary at the Department of Energy, quoted in Robert Pyper, *op. cit.,* p. 159.

24. Peter Kemp, 'A civil servant's view' in Dermot Englefield, ed., *Commons Select Committees. Catalysts for Progress?* (Longman, 1984), pp. 56–57.

25. Renee Short MP, then Chairman of the Select Committee on Social Services, quoted in Robert Pyper, *op. cit.*, p. 160.

26. Sir Douglas Wass, 'The public sector in modern society', *Public Administration*, Volume 61, Number 1, Spring 1983, p. 12.

27. *Ibid.*

28. For a full account, see Clive Ponting, *The Right To Know. The Inside Story of the Belgrano Affair* (Sphere, 1985).

29. For a discussion of these cases, see Robert Pyper, 'Sarah Tisdall, Ian Willmore and the civil servant's "right to leak"', *The Political Quarterly*, Volume 56, Number 1, January–March 1985.

30. Sir Douglas Wass, 'The civil service at the crossroads', *The Political Quarterly*, Volume 56, Number 3, July–September 1985.

31. This was reproduced as Appendix A to the Memorandum submitted by the Cabinet Office to the Treasury and Civil Service Committee, Seventh Report from the Treasury and Civil Service Committee, HC 92 1985–86.

32. Fourth Report from the Defence Committee, HC 519 1985–86.

33. Seventh Report from the Treasury and Civil Service Committee, *op. cit.*
34. HC Deb 6s 103 1985–86.
35. HC Deb 6s 123 1987–88 c572–575.

Chapter 5 Ethics in the Civil Service

1. Note of Guidance on the Duties and Responsibilities of Civil Servants in Relation to Ministers (the 'Armstrong Memorandum'), reproduced as Appendix A to the Memorandum submitted by the Cabinet Office to the Treasury and Civil Service Committee, Seventh Report from the Treasury and Civil Service Committee, HC 92 1985–86.
2. Gavin Drewry and Tony Butcher, *The Civil Service Today* (Basil Blackwell, 1988), pp. 188–9.
3. *Ibid.*
4. Eighth Report from the Treasury and Civil Service Committee, HC 302 1983–84.
5. Government observations on the Eighth Report from the Treasury and Civil Service Committee, Cmnd 9465.
6. Geoffrey K. Fry, *The Changing Civil Service* (Allen and Unwin, 1985) pp. 125–8.
7. Gavin Drewry and Tony Butcher, *op. cit.,* p. 124.
8. Raymond Fitzwalter and David Taylor, *Web of Corruption. The Story of J. G. L. Poulson and T. Dan Smith* (Granada, 1981), p. 127.
9. Report on the Property Services Agency by Sir Geoffrey Wardale for the Secretary of State for the Environment. This was published as Appendix D of the 26th Report from the House of Commons Committee of Public Accounts ('Fraud in the PSA: The Wardale Report') HC 295 1983–84.
10. Roy Gregory and Peter Hutchesson, *The Parliamentary Ombudsman* (Allen and Unwin, 1975), p. 64.
11. Report of the Tribunal appointed to inquire into certain issues arising out of the operations of the Crown Agents as financiers on own account in the years 1967–74 (Croom-Johnson Report), HC 364 1981–82.
12. Leader heading, *The Times*, 27 May 1982.
13. Report of the Tribunal appointed to inquire into certain issues in relation to the circumstances leading up to the cessation of

trading by the Vehicle and General Insurance Company Limited (the James Report), HC 133 1971–72. para 341.

14. *Ibid.*, paras 338–340.

15. Sir Antony Part, former Permanent Secretary at the Department of Trade and Industry, quoted in Robert Pyper, 'The doctrine of individual ministerial responsibility in British government: theory and practice in a new regime of parliamentary accountability, Ph.D. thesis, University of Leicester, 1987, p. 246.

16. HC Deb 5s 530 1953–54.

17. HC Deb 5s 836 1971–72 c72.

18. For a biting critique of the Tribunal, see R.J.S. Baker, 'The V and G affair and ministerial responsibility', *The Political Quarterly,* Volume 43, 1972.

19. HC Deb 5s 836 1971–72 c159.

20. Report of an Inquiry by HM Chief Inspector of Prisons into the Security Arrangements at HM Prison, Maze, HC 202 1983–84.

21. *The Times*, 8 February 1984.

22. Fourth Report from the Defence Committee 1985–86 HC 519, para 149

23. *Ibid.,* para 213.

24. *Constitutional Reform. The Quarterly Review*, Volume 4, Number 2, Summer 1989, p. 2.

25. In the discussion of this question, I have drawn heavily on Robert Pyper, 'Sarah Tisdall, Ian Willmore, and the civil servant's "right to leak"', *The Political Quarterly*, Volume 56, Number 1, January–March 1985.

26. For a discussion of the operation of 'open government' systems, see Rosamund Thomas: 'The experience of other countries' in Richard A. Chapman and Michael Hunt (eds), *Open Government* (Routledge, 1989). It should be noted that even the most 'open' system of government retains secrecy for some basic government functions. Even where rights of access to official information exist, the specific procedures to be followed by a person requesting information, the time limits within which government departments must disclose requested information, and the systems for appealing against denials of requests, all serve to complicate the supposed simplicity of government 'openness'.

27. Martin Gilbert: *Winston S. Churchill Volume 5, 1922–39* (Heinemann, 1976), p. 555. See also the *Companion* volumes which contain the Churchill–Morton correspondence.
28. See Robert Pyper (1985), *op. cit.*, for an analysis of the Tisdall and Willmore cases.
29. Clive Ponting,. *The Right To Know. The Inside Story of the Belgrano Affair* (Sphere, 1985), pp. 150–1.
30. See the Memoranda submitted by the FDA and the Council of Civil Service Unions, to the Treasury and Civil Service Committee, Seventh Report from the Treasury and Civil Service Committee HC 92 1985–86.
31. Sir Douglas Wass, 'The civil service at the crossroads', *The Political Quarterly*, Volume 56, Number 3, July–September 1985.
32. Appendix A to the Memorandum submitted by the Cabinet Office to the Treasury and Civil Service Committee, *op. cit.*
33. Clive Ponting, *Tragedy and Farce* (Sphere, 1986), p. 241.
34. Peter Wright, with Paul Greengrass, *Spycatcher* (Heinemann Australia, 1987).

Chapter 6 Managerialism and 'Efficiency'

1. C. H. Sisson, 'The civil service after Fulton' in W. J. Stankiewcz (ed.), *British Government in an Era of Reform* (Collier Macmillan, 1976), pp. 255–6.
2. 'Control of Public Expenditure' (Plowden Report), Cmnd 1432, 1961.
3. 'The Civil Service' (Fulton Report), Cmnd 3638, 1968.
4. Plowden Report, para 44.
5. See, for example, John Garrett, *Managing The Civil Service* (Heinemann, 1980), Chapter 2, and Sir James Dunnett, 'The civil service: seven years after Fulton', *Public Administration*, Volume 54, Number 4, 1976.
6. Civil Service Commission, Annual Report 1986 (HMSO, 1986).
7. 'The Reorganisation of Central Government', Cmnd 4506, 1970, para 3(ii).
8. HC Deb 5s 805 1970–71 c871–986.
9. Sir Richard Clarke, 'The number and size of government departments', *The Political Quarterly*, Volume 43, Number 2, 1972, p. 180.

10. Sir Patrick Nairne: 'Managing the DHSS Elephant: Reflections on a Giant Department', *The Political Quarterly*, Volume 54, Number 3, 1983, pp. 251–2.

11. Gavin Drewry and Tony Butcher, *The Civil Service Today* (Basil Blackwell, 1988), p. 197.

12. Andrew Gray and William I. Jenkins, *Administrative Politics in British Government* (Wheatsheaf, 1985), p. 106.

13. 'The Future of the Civil Service Department: Government Observations on the First Report from the Treasury and Civil Service Committee', Cmnd 8170, 1980–81.

14. Leslie Chapman, *Your Disobedient Servant* (Chatto and Windus, 1978).

15. Clive Ponting, *Whitehall: Tragedy and Farce* (Sphere, 1986), p. 215.

16. 'The Rayner Scrutiny Programmes 1979 to 1983', National Audit Office, HC 322 1985–86.

17. Early doubts along these lines were expressed in the Third Report from the Treasury and Civil Service Select Committee, HC 236 1981–82.

18. Clive Ponting, *Whitehall: Changing the Old Guard* (Unwin, 1989).

19. National Audit Office, *op. cit.*

20. Thirty-ninth Report from the Committee of Public Accounts, HC 365 1985–86.

21. Les Metcalfe and Sue Richards, *Improving Public Management* (Sage, second edition, 1990), p. 3.

22. Andrew Likierman, 'Management information for ministers: the MINIS system in the Department of the Environment', *Public Administration*, Volume 60, Number 2, 1982, p. 133.

23. Third Report from the Treasury and Civil Service Committee, 1981–82, *op. cit.*

24. Cmnd 8616, 1982.

25. See especially the 1983 White Paper, 'Financial Management in Government Departments', Cmnd 9058, 1983.

26. Les Metcalfe and Sue Richards, *op. cit.*, p. 216.

27. Clive Ponting, *Whitehall: Changing the Old Guard*, *op. cit.*, p. 69.

28. His lectures were subsequently published. See Sir John Hoskyns, 'Whitehall and Westminster: an outsider's view', *Parliamentary*

Affairs, Volume 36, Number 2, 1983, and Sir John Hoskyns, 'Conservatism is not enough', *The Political Quarterly*, Volume 55, Number 1, 1984.

29. Sir John Hoskyns, 'Whitehall and Westminster: an outsider's view', *op. cit.*, p. 140.

30. Douglas Wass, 'The public service in modern society', *Public Administration*, Volume 61, Number 1, 1983, p. 13.

31. Sir Patrick Nairne, 'Great Britain Limited', *The Sunday Times*, 2 October 1983.

32. Gavin Drewry and Tony Butcher, *op. cit.*, p. 110.

33. Review of Personnel Work in the Civil Service: Report to the Prime Minister (Cassels Report) 1983.

34. For an account of this episode, see Peter Hennessy, *Whitehall* (Secker and Warburg, 1989) pp. 371–3.

35. Seventh Report from the Treasury and Civil Service Committee, HC 92 1985–86 paras 5.13, 5.18.

36. RIPA, *Top Jobs in Whitehall* (RIPA, 1987), p. 61.

Chapter 7 Beyond Whitehall

1. 'The Dispersal of Government Work from London' (Hardman Report) Cmnd 5332, 1973.

2. For a discussion of the early phase of this revolution, see D. C. Pitt and B. C. Smith (eds), *The Computer Revolution in British Public Administration* (Wheatsheaf, 1984).

3. Peter Hennessy, 'Mandarins thirst for revolution', *The Independent*, 23 October 1989.

4. Civil Service Commission, Annual Report, 1988.

5. *The Times*, 15 November 1989.

6. 'The Civil Service' (Fulton Report) Cmnd 3638, 1968.

7. Cmnd 4506, 1970.

8. Peter Hennessy, *Whitehall* (Secker and Warburg, 1989).

9. 'Report on Non-Departmental Public Bodies' (Pliatzky Report) Cmnd 7797, 1980.

10. Figures taken from John Greenwood and David Wilson, *Public Administration in Britain Today* (Unwin Hyman, 2nd Edition, 1989).

11. Terms of reference are set out in: Efficiency Unit, *Improving Management In Government: The Next Steps* (HMSO, 1988).

12. *Ibid.*, para 10.

13. *Ibid.*, para 19.
14. *Ibid.*, Annex A, para 3.
15. *Ibid.*, para 41.
16. Gavin Drewry, 'Forward from FMI: 'The Next Steps'', *Public Law*, Winter 1988.
17. HC Deb 6s 127 c1149–1156.
18. Eighth Report from the Treasury and Civil Service Committee, HC 494 1987–88.
19. See H. M. Treasury, *Pay and Management Flexibilities* (Treasury, August 1989).
20. 'The Financing and Accountability of Next Steps Agencies', Cmnd 914, 1989–90.
21. Butler's speech was reported in *The Guardian*, 21 September 1988.
22. Eighth Report from the Treasury and Civil Service Committee, *op. cit.*, para 7.
23. *Ibid.*, paras 46 and 47.
24. *Ibid.*, para 49.
25. 'Civil Service Management Reform: The Next Steps', The Government's Response to the Eighth Report from the Treasury and Civil Service Committee (HMSO, 1988).
26. Eighth Report from the Treasury and Civil Service Committee, HC 481 1989–90.
27. *Ibid.*, paras 68 and 70.

Select Bibliography

The Notes and References for each chapter give details of the important books, articles and documents relating to each of the topics examined. What follows here is simply a brief summary of key works of a general nature. It should be remembered that sources of information on the civil service are wide and varied, and this is by no means a definitive list. Students at all levels who are required to answer examination questions on the civil service must have the ability to illustrate general themes with reference to particular illustrative examples and academic debates. Journals such as *Talking Politics*, *Social Studies Review*, *The Political Quarterly*, *Parliamentary Affairs* and *Public Administration* are particularly useful for this purpose.

Gavin Drewry and Tony Butcher, *The Civil Service Today* (Basil Blackwell, 1988).

Geoffrey K. Fry, *The Changing Civil Service* (Allen and Unwin, 1985).

Andrew Gray and William I. Jenkins, *Administrative Politics in British Government* (Wheatsheaf, 1985).

Peter Hennessy, *Cabinet* (Basil Blackwell, (1986).

Peter Hennessy, *Whitehall* (Secker and Warburg, 1989).

Peter Kellner and Lord Crowther-Hunt, *The Civil Servants. An Inquiry into Britain's Ruling Class* (Macdonald, 1980).

Les Metcalfe and Sue Richards, *Improving Public Management* (Sage, second edition, 1990).

Clive Ponting, *The Right To Know. The Inside Story of the Belgrano Affair* (Sphere, 1985).

Clive Ponting, *Whitehall: Tragedy and Farce* (Sphere, 1986).

Clive Ponting, *Whitehall: Changing The Old Guard* (Unwin, 1989).

Royal Institute of Public Administration, *Future Shape of Reform in Whitehall* (RIPA, 1988).

Royal Institute of Public Administration, *Top Jobs in Whitehall. Appointments and Promotions in the Senior Civil Service* (RIPA, 1987).

Hugo Young and Anne Sloman, *No, Minister. An Inquiry into the Civil Service* (BBC, 1982).

Hugo Young and Anne Sloman, *But, Chancellor. An Inquiry into the Treasury* (BBC, 1984).

Index